JUICE IT UP!

Pat Gentry
with
Lynne Devereux

101 PRODUCTIONS

Publisher	Brete C. Harrison
Associate Publisher	James Connolly
Editor	Annette Gooch
Proofreader	Carolyn Chandler
Editorial Assistant	Nicole Aronescu
Director of Production	Steve Lux
Interior Designers	Steve Lux and Octavo
Illustrator	Glenda Berg
Cover Design	Glenn Martinez & Associates
Cover Photography	Michael Lamotte

None of the information in this book is intended to replace the recommendations of a qualified health care provider. Any application of information in this book is at the reader's discretion and sole responsibility.

Nutritional Analysis Chart based on *Calories/Nutrient Counter* from Heizer Software, Pleasant Hill, Calif., © 1989, by Peter G. Canonico.

Printed and bound in the USA
Published by 101 Productions/The Cole Group
4415 Sonoma Highway, PO Box 4089
Santa Rosa, CA 95402-4089

Distributed to the book trade by Publishers Group West
and to the gift and gourmet trade by Max Burton Enterprises, Inc.

C D E F G H
2 3 4 5 6 7 8 9

ISBN 1-56426-507-2

To my husband, companion,
friend and willing tester,
I dedicate this book. Life has its
ups and downs but he has
always been there to "smooth"
the rough edges.

CONTENTS

INTRODUCTION

M ost of us were introduced to juice as children, when it was a welcome addition to our limited beverage choices. I remember hot Oregon summers when my mother would make tall icy pitchers of lemonade garnished with mint leaves. Sometimes she added gingerale and made lemonade spritzers, which she then served to us with cookies or light little cakes. This was the era of colored glass pitchers and matching beverage glasses from the 1930s and 1940s. "Depression glass," as it was called, often appeared with lemonade and cake, or with brewed iced tea and finger sandwiches as an afternoon repast.

Orange juice became the answer to including fruit and vitamin C for breakfast, and orange juice concentrate was the quickest means to that end. What a leap away we made from the freshly squeezed juice of a sweet orange! Canned juices gave us possibilities for eternal storage, but the essence of fruit taste and nutrition was lost in the canning process. All along, a small group of health enthusiasts and juice bar afficionados have extolled the benefits of fresh ripe food juiced and served in imaginative combinations with taste and nutrition still intact.

We now enter an era of new dietary goals. Fiber, minerals, vitamins, natural sugar and low sodium are vital concerns in planning our daily meals. Support for organically grown produce and meats is growing as we demand chemical-free foods. The neighborhood produce market and seasonal farmers markets are teeming with varieties of foods grown locally and flown in fresh from faraway fields. For those of us who garden or stalk the farmers markets for the freshest possible foods, a juice extractor turns the ripe vegetables and fruits into more than thirst-quenching drinks.

What a delight it is to extract the juice of tree-ripened apricots, peaches, plums and nectarines and include the juice in recipes for added flavor. Marinades, sauces, soups, dressings and desserts all benefit from the juicy essence extracted from fresh fruits and vegetables.

Whether you're an athlete, a parent with children who need to watch sugar intake, or an everyday brown-bagger who is careful about the meals you take to work, you will find creative new ways to make your meals perfect pleasures. Juices and meals made with your juicer will contain only the amounts of salt, sugar and fat that you add yourself.

I can truly say I've had fun using my juice extractor and look forward to years of nutrition and taste treats from fresh juices. I hope the recipes in this book will inspire you to create combinations using foods that are your own particular passion. Whether your creation is sipped from a frosty mug, a warm steamy thermos or an elegant goblet by candlelight, I wish you pleasure and good health when you *Juice It Up!*

JUICE REAMERS AND EXTRACTORS

Juice Reamers

Among my antique cookware collection is a hand-held wooden reamer. It is a conical, ridged utensil made to extract juice from citrus fruits. In looking at it, I can see the evolution it followed from wood to metal, then glass, and recently into an electrical appliance.

The electric reamer works by a relatively simple process and is a wonderful improvement over its wooden ancestor. Movement of the cone is triggered by pressing downward on half a citrus fruit placed on the cone. The machine turns off when pressure is released.

My first electric reamer was a Mother's Day gift from my daughter. We had a prolific backyard lemon tree and a family fondness for lemonade, lemon curd, and lemon meringue pie. Fruit from our lemon tree was bountiful, and I wanted to squeeze and use all the lemon juice. I always set aside time to "ream" lemon juice and freeze it. The distinctive taste of fresh lemon juice made all of our lemon creations special.

Juice Extractors

Juice extractors first appeared primarily in health food stores. They were expensive, bulky, and used to produce a limited array of drinks in large quantities. The exceptional nutritional value of freshly extracted juice led to experiments with varieties and combinations of foods, and improved technology of the juice extractor. Today's compact, highly efficient extractors are made for convenient, smaller servings.

The predominant machine in today's market is the juice extractor. Pieces of fruits and vegetables are pushed through a tubular chute similar to that of a food processor. A round strainer filter basket with very fine grating teeth whirls as it grates the fruits or vegetables, creating both juice and pulp. The pulp is forced up and out of the filter basket into a pulp basket or container. Juice is forced through the filter, along a downspout and into a juice receptacle. Some manufacturers provide a juice receptacle with the machine.

Also available are some combination extractor/reamers that use an interchangeable reamer mechanism for citrus fruits and an extractor strainer for other fruits and vegetables. Most extractors also process peeled citrus fruits, however.

Fresh juice is the primary product of extractors and the secondary product is pulp. Some of the pulp can be incorporated into sauces, dips, pasta and bakery products. But a large percentage consists of very fibrous matter, seeds and skin, making it largely unuseable. Gardeners may wish to use some of the pulp in composting.

In testing the various juice machines, I set up my work area with the juice extractor, a blender and a mini-chopper. Having these three appliances grouped together made processing juice and combination drinks quick and easy. My electric mixer was close at hand for preparing desserts and baked items. I used the mini-chopper frequently for ingredients used in a finely chopped form. Smoothies and other milk-based drinks were best when whipped in the blender or with the immersion blender.

I also included in my work area a slightly raised cutting board and a sharp knife. A certain amount of cutting and preparation is necessary prior to extracting juice. General guidelines for preparation are outlined in the Techniques and Tips section.

Testing extractors and creating new juice drinks has been

a creative and exciting process. Many times I started by first gathering the fruits or vegetables I had on hand or from the garden, and simply processing juice and experimenting with combinations. Find your own spirit of adventure. Try different and unusual combinations, using the best ingredients available. You will be rewarded with the refreshing tastes of healthful foods easily prepared.

TECHNIQUES AND TIPS

In this section are techniques that evolved as I developed recipes and tested various reamers, extractors, and combination extractor/reamers. Some of the techniques were suggested in booklets packaged by the manufacturers but many of them came from experimenting with fresh foods in sensible and economical preparations for juicing.

Remember to choose the freshest and finest ingredients available, not the most expensive. (You can adjust the recipe if one of the items called for is not at its best.) Consume the juice as soon as possible after processing for maximum vitamin retention.

Preparation

1. Use the freshest ingredients, preferably produce that has not been sprayed with insecticides.
2. Wash fruits and vegetables well. Whatever is left on the produce (dirt, insects, etc.) will be processed into juice.
3. Peel and core fruits and vegetables if you plan on using the resulting pulp in bakery goods or sauces. The pulp will have a more even consistency.
4. Cut produce into pieces that fit the feed tube. Firm produce such as carrots should be cut into 1 ½-inch pieces.

5. Remove outer rind and seeds from melons. Remove rind and hard core from pineapple.
6. Citrus processed with the extractor must have outer peel removed. The white membrane, which is high in nutritional content, can be discarded or processed, according to individual preference. Large seeds should also be removed.
7. Leafy produce (lettuce, cabbage, spinach, etc.) should be rolled into cylinders before being placed into feed tube.
8. Fibrous or stringy produce (celery, leeks, green onions) should be cut crosswise into ½-inch to 1-inch pieces. (Some manufacturers recommend against using rhubarb.)
9. Remove stones (pits) from apricots, plums, peaches and nectarines. Remove stems from grapes.

Process

1. Follow manufacturers' instructions in operating equipment.
2. If citrus is being processed and you are working with an extractor/reamer, ream the citrus juice first, then proceed with extraction.
3. In combination drinks calling for a thick nectar or purée, process these first, then process fruits producing thinner juice.
4. When processing garlic or fresh herbs such as parsley and watercress for combination drinks, process these along with larger pieces of produce. (Alternate items as you feed them into feed tube.)
5. To process, turn machine on first, be sure basket is rotating properly and then add produce through the feed tube. Slowly process food, using the pusher. As a safety measure, always use the food pusher to guide produce into feed tube.

6. Listen for any change in the noise level of your machine or for a sound indicating the machine is slowing down. If necessary, turn machine off, unplug and check pulp container and underside of lid. Leafy produce and moist pulp will tend to build up. Simply remove excess pulp, and replug machine and proceed with juice extraction.

7. When juicing is completed, switch machine to off; allow basket to stop.

8. Manufacturers consistently advise unplugging machine upon completion of juice extraction before proceeding with disassembling and cleanup.

9. When processing large quantities of juice, check level of juice receptacle to avoid overflow.

10. Add a few teaspoons of lemon juice to retain fresh color in juices that are light in color (peach, apricot, nectarine, mango).

11. It is natural for some pulp to remain in the juice.

Clean-up

1. NOT ALL MANUFACTURERS RECOMMEND DISH-WASHER USE FOR CLEAN-UP. Extreme heat of dishwashers could cause plastic parts to warp and become misaligned.

2. For the conservation-wise consumer, empty pulp into a container, bury in the garden or add to the compost pile. Rinse juicer parts with garden hose over flower beds.

3. At the kitchen sink, rinse off juicer parts, using warm water. Use a stiff brush (a toothbrush works well) to remove particles of pulp from strainer basket.

4. Air- or towel-dry juicer parts.

Safety

Manufacturers generally concur on the following safety recommendations:

1. Read the instruction booklet carefully before operating equipment.
2. Do not allow children to operate equipment or to be nearby when equipment is in use.
3. Do not immerse motor housing in water. Wipe off with a damp cloth.
4. Be sure juicer cover is thoroughly locked into place before turning on motor.
5. Do not use appliances outdoors.
6. Be sure electric cord is not damaged and do not allow cord to hang over counter edge.
7. Be sure off/on switch is turned off and basket has ceased rotating before removing lid.
8. Do not put fingers into feed tube. Use food pusher at all times.
9. Do not leave juicer unattended while in use.
10. Handle strainer basket carefully. It has sharp grating edges.

JUICE INGREDIENTS

Fresh! Fresh! Fresh! You will want to use the freshest of ingredients at their optimum stage of ripeness, ripe but firm. The flavor and the vitamin and mineral content are at their best in fresh produce selected at its peak.

Certain ingredients will prevail in your selection. The most popular vegetables I relied on were carrots, tomatoes, bell peppers, cucumbers, leeks and green onions, beets, basil, dill, parsley and watercress.

When I began developing the recipes for the juice extractors, it was early June, so I started with the berries, followed by stone fruits (apricots, cherries, plums, nectarines and peaches). Grapes and pineapples were readily available and so were cold storage apples. As fall grew near I processed freshly picked apples.

My favorite fruits for juicing seemed to be pineapple, raspberries, strawberries, nectarines, peaches and apricots. Citrus juices were used as juice components, flavor enhancers and color preservers.

Early in the testing, I started getting up early on Saturdays to shop at the Certified Farmer's market held at our local community college. Much of the produce available there is produced by certified organic farmers and is grown without the use of pesticides. I also found, particularly with the berry growers, that the produce is picked at the last possible moment. The flavor was fantastic, fresh and sweet and rich.

Having lived in the Santa Clara Valley when it was a prime cherry and apricot growing area (prior to being turned into Silicon Valley), we had three apricot trees. The fruit from these trees spoiled me for life. So I knew that if I wanted tree- ripened apricots, I would have to get them directly from the grower or at the farmer's market. I was not disappointed; local farmers and also some who "live around the hill" in the Gilroy area brought in the best.

The local agricultural commissioner's office was helpful in supplying guidelines for both certified organic farmers and certified farmers' markets. The following summarizes what I feel consumers need to know about produce grown and sold under these specifications. The following are required:

1. No pesticides used
2. Only organic fertilizers used
3. Carefully kept records indicating all organic materials added and any allowed sprays used (how much, date of use)

4. Description of plot of agricultural parcel certified as organic; registration with the county agricultural office

Juice Ingredients to Plant in Your Home Garden

Climate and geographical location, and available garden space will play a large part in determining what items you can grow in your home garden. As a resident of California, I have to remember that I live in an agricultural oasis. Because the coastal area where I live does receive a winter chill but generally has a warm spring and reasonably hot summer, a wide range of fruits and vegetables grows well in my area.

Produce items requiring hotter summers are grown in adjacent areas and trucked in daily. Also, the west coast generally has a steady supply of the tropical fruits and produce from the Pacific Rim countries.

Listed below are fruits and vegetables that seemed to be most appealing for juicing. Fresh herbs, of course, are high on the list of items to plant.

Fruit Trees
Apple
Apricot
Cherry
Lemon
Lime
Nectarine
Orange
Peach
Plum

Berries
Strawberries
Raspberries
Blackberries

Row Crops
Beets
Cabbage
Carrots
Celery
Cucumbers
Green onions (scallions)
Leeks
Lettuce
Peppers (bell and jalapeño)
Spinach
Tomatoes

Herbs
Basil
Chervil
Chives
Dill
Marjoram
Mint
Parsley
Pineapple sage
Rosemary
Tarragon
Thyme
Watercress

Melons
Cantaloupe
Honeydew
Watermelon

JUICE DRINKS

I use the term juice to mean a mixture of juices, a blending of flavors that will give you variety and economy in using your juicer. Since many of the new generation of juice extractors are meant to produce single servings extracted directly into a glass, most recipes listed serve one person. The recipes can be easily doubled or tripled, but just be sure you have a large enough receptacle under the spout to receive the juice.

I recommend that you use frozen juice concentrates when certain fruits are out of season or are prohibitively expensive. For instance, adding a small amount of a tropical juice such as coconut or tamarind to a punch or party drink can give it a special flavor. Most of the drinks can be sweetened naturally by including a small piece of apple or a handful of grapes during processing, but you can also use honey, brown rice syrup, fructose or maple syrup.

Vegetable drinks can benefit from a dash of salt or seasoning salt to enhance the flavor, but you can keep your drinks salt-free by adding small amounts of lemon juice or processing fresh herbs with the vegetables. Unfortunately, not all vegetables lend themselves to juicing. Asparagus, broccoli, cauliflower, squash and some leafy greens produced bitter or astringent juices, and I like them much better served as steamed vegetables. I processed potato juice and used it very successfully as a thickener in soups. This will be one for you to experiment with.

I find that most juice drinks taste best if served slightly chilled. Serve them over ice, or use chilled produce to make your juice. For the maximum nutritional benefit, serve your drinks fresh from the juicer. Most important, choose the freshest ingredients possible. The abundance and variety of foods available to us each season mean that our juicers need never be idle.

FRUIT JUICES

APRICOT BLUSH

6 apricots
¼ pint berries (half of one ½-pint box: raspberries, blackberries, or other berries)

"Summertime, and the living is easy..." and the fruit is abundant, and the flavors are golden gifts of the sun for eight or ten glorious weeks. To truly consume summer, use the market's best offering of glowing peaches; ripe, juicy nectarines or downy, golden apricots. Pick the best berries you can find to make a riotous drink of summer fruits.

I've chosen apricots to go with the berries, offering a special toast to the brief season of great apricots. Feel free to celebrate with the fruit of your choice.

Makes 1 serving, 6 ounces

Extract juice, combine and serve. You can make this drink into a spritzer by adding some seltzer or sparkling mineral water.

THE BLUSHING PEAR

½ cup pear juice
¼ cup cherry, strawberry, or
raspberry juice
1 or 2 drops almond extract
(optional)

Making a sweet little pear blush would not be hard if you had one of these bold red fruits accompany it. In ancient Christian tradition the almond tree was symbolic of the Virgin Mary, so adding a drop or two of almond extract could help restore a bit of purity. This juice is a nutritious, fat-free way to indulge in the flavor of those pear and cherry pies with the lovely fragrance of almond extract that Mom used to make. Be sure to make more if company's coming.

Makes 1 serving, 6 ounces

Combine juices.

PEAR PLUM SWEET-TART

1 pear, cut to fit feed tube
2 plums, cut in half, pits
removed
2 tablespoons orange juice
(juice of ½ orange)
½ teaspoon sugar (optional)

There comes a time in midsummer when markets are overwhelmed with plums. Varieties, colors, shapes and sizes vary as you nibble your way through the season. Early on, try to get the Santa Rosa plums for your first juice of the summer. Around the middle of July you see the yellow Wicksons and black-skinned Friars. By August, treat yourself to the Queen Ann, by far the finest and juiciest variety of the summer. Whatever variety is your local specialty, be ready when they all ripen at once.

Skins of plums are tart and might leave the juice wanting a sweetener. A ripe pear and a bit of orange juice give this recipe a satisfying balance of sweet and tart.

Makes 1 serving, 8 ounces

Extract juice from pear and plums. Add orange juice and sugar, if used. Stir to combine.

PINEAPPLE GRAPEFRUIT JUICE

¼ pineapple, peeled, cored,
  and cut to fit feed tube
1 grapefruit, rind removed
  and sectioned, or ⅓ cup
  reamed grapefruit juice
1 teaspoon sugar, or
  handful of grapes,
  processed (optional)

This recipe calls for real pineapple, flown in daily from Hawaii and combined with mainland grapefruits to form a sweet, tangy tropical union. Since excellent grapefruit is available from October through May and pineapple nearly year-round, this drink can be a vitamin ritual morning, noon and evening.

Makes 1 serving, 7 ounces

Extract juice and add sugar if desired. Pour over ice and serve.

AMBROSIAL DELIGHT

¼ pineapple, peeled, cored
  and cut to fit feed tube
½ apple, cut to fit feed tube
3 tablespoons orange juice
2 to 3 tablespoons coconut
  milk (page 21)
½ banana

The word *ambrosia,* from a Greek root meaning *immortal,* was used to describe foods set before Greek and Roman gods. Perhaps the gods nourished their godly immortality with exotic nectars of pineapples, oranges, apples and bananas. But it's the addition of coconut that makes the modern palate say *ambrosia.* In the time it takes to flip on your juicer and peel a banana you can prepare a divine offering that will conjure sea breezes and an endless afternoon.

Makes 1 serving, 10 ounces

Extract juice from pineapple and apple. Combine with remaining ingredients, using a blender or immersion blender.

MINTED BLUEBERRY "DEW"

½ cup blueberries
¼ honeydew melon, rind and
    seeds removed, cut to fit
    feed tube
¼ cup green grapes, stems
    removed
3 or 4 mint leaves

Fortune brought a mild winter, relatively speaking, the one year I lived in Chicago, followed by a long, warm spring and summer. One of the biggest treats on summer Saturdays was a caravan of trucks bearing fresh vegetables and fruits grown by neighboring farmers in Michigan and Illinois. The Farmer's Market was a gathering of devoted Midwestern growers and their hard-earned bounty of fresh corn, brussels sprouts, precious peaches, and the jewel in Michigan's crown, blueberries. I took home at least a flat of berries each week, not an easy trick on my trusty bicycle.

Blueberries mean summer to me, even if I pull them from the freezer in February. Here, you can blend blueberries with honeydew melon (which provides the "dew" in this recipe), grapes, and a hint of mint for a perfect combination of cool colors and thirst-quenching juices.

Makes 1 serving, 6 ounces

Extract juice from fruit. Process mint leaves as you add fruit.

SUMMER HARVEST

2 apricots, pits removed
½ peach, pit removed, cut to
    fit feed tube
½ nectarine, pit removed, cut
    to fit feed tube
1 plum, pit removed, cut to fit
    feed tube
½ pint raspberries

When summer's bounty is at its peak, it's hard to choose from among the scrumptious, juicy offerings of a farmer's market or roadside stand. Celebrate by making a summer harvest drink with all your favorite fruits. My weakness for apricots and raspberries led me to this rewarding recipe.

Makes 1 serving, 6 ounces

Extract juice from fruit. Stir and serve. For thinner juice, add spring water.

AUTUMN HARVEST

1 apple, cut in pieces to fit
    feed tube
1 pear, cut in pieces to fit
    feed tube
½ cup tokay or muscat
    grapes, stems removed
Dash of nutmeg (optional)

When fall sends out its signals of nippy weather and colorful leaves, I think of pumpkins growing plump on vines and the ripening fruits of fall. Apples, pears, and tokay or muscat grapes combine here to herald the autumn harvest. Nutmeg gives a dash to apples and pears anytime.

Makes 1 serving, 10 ounces

Extract juice from fruit. Stir and pour into glass. Sprinkle with dash of nutmeg if desired.

APPLE STRAWBERRY DELIGHT

1 pint strawberries, hulls
    removed
1 apple, cut to fit feed tube

You will find no resemblance in this drink to commercially prepared, sugary apple-berry drinks. This is the flavor and nutrition of fresh fruit prepared and enjoyed expediently. Make it for your family's lunch for a boost from *real* fruit.

Makes 1 serving, 8 ounces

Extract juice from fruit. Stir and serve.

CRANAPPLE SPLASH

1 apple, quartered
1 cup cranberries
½ cup grapes

Tart and tangy with just a hint of sweetness from the grape juice, this is a fall treat. Cranberries produce a beautiful crimson-colored juice that can also be used in a flavorful punch for the holidays.

Makes 1 serving, 6 ounces

Extract juice from fruit; stir to combine. Serve well chilled.

PINK ZINGER

Seeds of 1 pomegranate
1 pear, quartered
½ cup red grapes
Juice of 1 orange

Pomegranate juice has long been a favorite of mine. It combines well with other fruit juice, adding a unique flavor with a tart finish. I also like to use pomegranate juice in meat marinades.

Note that the seeds will rattle around as you extract the juice, and you may need to strain the extracted juice.

Makes 1 serving, 9 ounces

Extract juice from pomegranate, pear and grapes. Combine with orange juice and serve.

OVER THE RAINBOW

½ pint strawberries, hulls
    removed
1 peach, pit removed, cut to
    fit feed tube
2 apricots, pits removed
½ pint blueberries
1 kiwi, peeled, cut to fit feed
    tube

Think of the colors of a rainbow and you'll find my inspiration for this drink. The pot of gold at this rainbow's end is a wealth of vitamins and minerals.

Makes 2 servings, 12 ounces

Extract juice. Stir and serve chilled.

THE SETTING SUN

1 nectarine, pit removed, cut
    to fit feed tube
½ pint raspberries
2 tablespoons orange juice

Here is a drink that has red, orange and yellow hues, with mellow flavors to savor at day's end.

Makes 1 serving, 5 ounces

Extract juice from fruit. Add orange juice and stir.

MELON MEDLEY

¼ watermelon, rind removed,
    cut to fit feed tube
½ casaba or Crenshaw melon,
    rind removed, cut to fit
    feed tube
2 tablespoons orange juice
Fresh mint leaves, for garnish

This is a perfect drink to make with pieces of different melons. If you've made melon balls, you can process the leftover melon. Flavors will blend to give you an essential melon taste.

Makes 1 serving, 7-8 ounces

Extract juice from melon. Add orange juice and stir. Serve in a tall glass with ice. Or, for a slightly different taste, pour over frozen tamarindade cubes (page 39).

FIRE AND ICE

½ **small watermelon or**
  ¼ **large watermelon**
½ **jalapeño pepper, seeds**
  removed

For many years, my husband has salted and lightly peppered his servings of watermelon. While processing some watermelon for juice, he suggested including a jalapeño pepper and created a chilly melon drink with a firey finish.

Makes 1 serving, 8 ounces

Extract juice. Serve well chilled.

HARVEST GLOW

6 **ounces cranberries**
  (½ package)
½ **pear, stem removed**
½ **cup red grapes**
1 **teaspoon simple syrup,**
  page 43 (optional)

Most of us crave cranberries around the holidays. Although fresh cranberries appear in the fall, they freeze beautifully and can be a staple in your diet year round. Cranberries have a full complement of vitamins and minerals in addition to their bright color and tart taste. This drink has a deep red cranberry color, with sweetness provided by grapes and pear.

Makes 1 serving, 6 ounces

Extract juice. Add simple syrup if desired. Stir and serve chilled or over ice.

FRESH COCONUT MILK

Island cultures have built their cuisines around coconuts for centuries, and built their homes with the leaves and trunks. But for many of us, opening a coconut is a lethal event. All it really takes is a sharp tool, a small knife and the imagination to see a monkey's face on that hairy shell. The shell actually protects a seed, which we eat as coconut meat, and from which we get coconut milk. If you puncture one of the "eyes" and then make a cut in the soft area that looks like a mouth, you will be rewarded with pure coconut water. This liquid is combined with grated coconut meat to make coconut milk.

To prepare fresh coconut milk, puncture, drain and crack one coconut. With a cleaver or hammer crack open the coconut. Remove the meat, taking off any brown skin. Cut meat in ½-inch cubes. For each cup of cubes, add ¾ cup hot water plus the reserved liquid. Purée the flesh and liquid in the blender for 30 seconds. Steep the mixture for 30 minutes and strain through a double thickness of cheese cloth. You will have about 2½ cups liquid. Any leftover coconut milk can be frozen in ice cube trays for future use.

Here are some combinations using coconut milk.

Each recipe makes two 6-ounce servings.

COCONUT TANGERINE

¼ cup coconut milk
1 tablespoon lime juice
1 cup tangerine juice
1 tablespoon sugar

COCONUT, ORANGE, PAPAYA

¼ cup coconut milk
½ cup orange juice
½ cup papaya nectar
1 tablespoon sugar

COCONUT PINEAPPLE

¼ cup coconut milk
1 cup pineapple juice
1 tablespoon lime juice
1 tablespoons sugar

COCONUT PEACH

¼ cup coconut milk
1 cup peach juice
2 tablespoons orange juice
1 tablespoon sugar

Combine juices for drink selected. Serve well chilled.

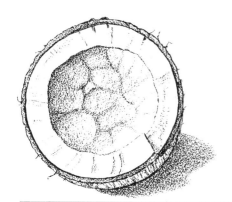

TROPICAL SUN

**1 mango, pit removed, cut to
fit feed tube**
**¼ pineapple, peeled, cored,
cut to fit feed tube**
**¼ cup coconut milk
(page 21)**
**1 to 2 tablespoons guava or
passion fruit frozen con-
centrate**

Touring the island of Oahu, we enjoyed the roadside stands selling local produce. Since guava and passion fruit are hardly local produce for most of us, and expensive when we do find them, I specify frozen concentrates for this recipe. Most of them are well prepared, with no additives. They give your drink a truly exotic flavor for a dream trip to faraway islands.

Makes 1 serving, 8 ounces

Extract juice from fruits. Stir in coconut milk and frozen concentrate. Pour over ice, in tall glass.

RED, WHITE AND BLUE

¼ cup strawberry juice
¼ cup coconut milk
¼ cup blueberry juice
**1 teaspoon simple syrup
(page 43)**

For many years I have planted pots with red, white and blue flowers, timing them to bloom on the 4th of July. This year, being in a festive mood, I hung out the flag and decided to combine these red, white, and blue ingredients. The resulting drink is a lovely shade of deep lavender. What a great way to accompany the barbecue and fireworks of a summer holiday.

Makes 1 serving, 6 ounces

Combine juice, coconut milk and simple syrup.

VEGETABLE JUICES

VITA COCKTAIL

2 tomatoes, cut to fit feed tube
1 carrot, cut to fit feed tube
Few sprigs of parsley
¼ red bell pepper
2 green onions, cut crosswise
    into 1-inch pieces
3 cabbage leaves, rolled into a
    cylinder
8 sprigs watercress
Dash of seasoning salt
    (optional)

You'll want to use the freshest vegetables you can obtain for this succulent taste of the garden. For a little dash of spice, add a jalapeño chile.

Makes 1 serving, 8 ounces

Extract juice from all ingredients alternately and continuously. Stir. Season with salt and pour over ice, if desired.

T.N.T. COCKTAIL

1 tomato, cut to fit feed tube
1 nectarine, cut to fit feed
    tube
2 tangerines, peeled, or
    ¼ cup juice made from
    frozen concentrate
1 tsp sugar or 1-2 tablespoons
    grape juice, as sweetener
    (optional)

Both nectarines and tangerines have potent, memorable fragrances. Nectarines are packed with vitamin C and tangerines contribute vitamin A. With a tomato included, this is a perfect morning juice. When tangerines are not in season, you may use frozen concentrated tangerine juice. During the winter months when the effervescent tangerine is available, you should be able to locate nectarines from South America. Try it some morning as a special wake-up drink.

Makes 1 serving, 6 ounces

Extract juice from tomato, nectarine and tangerines. Add sweetener if desired. Stir to combine.

IT'S ITALIAN

**3 Italian plum tomatoes, cut
  into quarters**
¼ green bell pepper
**2 or 3 scallions, cut crosswise
  into ½-inch pieces**
**2 to 4 fresh basil leaves,
  shredded**
Seasoning salt (optional)

In a customs dispute over a 10 percent duty slapped on a shipment of tomatoes from the West Indies, the United States Supreme Court declared the tomato to be forever a vegetable. But when my children are popping handfuls of sweet, juicy, vine-ripened cherry tomatoes into their mouths as we pick them, I don't dare tell them what the Court has ruled. Whether you grow them yourself or have a favorite farmer's market where you know loving care helped produce them, tomatoes are one of summer's chief joys. There is no comparison between the fruit of the vines and the gas-reddened, insipid product found in the produce section of our markets during winter months. By whatever means, make this vegetable a staple in your juice pantry.

In this recipe, the natural vitamin C, mineral and fiber content of tomatoes combine with the savory flavors of green bell pepper and fresh basil to create an Italian juice bonanza. Sip this after an early morning jog, relaxing in your favorite hammock. Or, try it as a pick-me-up some afternoon when guests are coming and you need to vacuum the whole house.

Makes 1 serving, 6 ounces

Place all ingredients in feed tube and extract juice.

Add a dash of salt to taste. Chill. Pour into juice glass and sprinkle top with basil shreds and dash of seasoning salt if desired.

PETER RABBIT'S SPECIAL

1 carrot, cut in pieces to fit
feed tube
1 stalk celery, strings removed
and cut into ½-inch pieces
3 cabbage leaves rolled into a
cylinder
3 or 4 sprigs of parsley
Dash of salt (optional)

Perhaps if Peter Rabbit had stayed with the recipe for this special juice, he could have avoided his mother's chiding and the dose of chamomile tea. Carrots, cabbage and celery are all excellent digestive aids. Carrots are packed with vitamins A and C, and celery contributes significant calcium to this lovely garden drink. If you like to experiment, try some of the Chinese varieties of cabbage. They tend to be spicier than the domestic kind, so will add some zip to your drink.

Makes 1 serving, 6 ounces

Continuously feed vegetables through feed tube. Stir juice; season with salt if desired.

TIGER TOM

2 Roma tomatoes, cut to fit
feed tube
1 carrot, cut to fit feed tube
½ jalapeño pepper and ½ teaspoon sugar or ½ teaspoon
Tiger Sauce
Dash of salt (optional)

You could consider Tiger Tom a counterpart to a Bloody Mary. Both are adept at giving us that weekend wake-up call while providing some vitamins at the same time. This version of Tiger Tom does not use vodka, aquavit or tequila, but if the occasion presents itself, do experiment. Roasting the jalapeños slightly before juicing gives the drink a smokey flavor and softens the skin of the pepper.

The gourmet section of some markets carries a bottled hot sauce called Tiger Sauce. You can substitute ½ teaspoon of Tiger Sauce for the jalapeño pepper if desired.

Makes 1 serving, 6 ounces

Extract juice from tomatoes, carrot and jalapeño. Season with salt if desired.

SUMMER SALAD IN A GLASS

6 lettuce leaves, rolled into
cylinders
6 spinach leaves, rolled into
cylinders
2 tomatoes, cut to fit feed tube
Fresh basil or dill, a few leaves
or sprigs
1 green onion, cut into 1-inch
pieces
½ green or red bell pepper
½ carrot, cut to fit feed tube
Dash of salt or seasoning salt

There are times in summer when it's easy to indulge in a bountiful farmer's market or produce stand and bring home more fresh food than you can consume as salad or cooked vegetables. If you're an ambitious gardener, your own refrigerator won't hold all that is harvested at peak season. This is the perfect time to "juice it up." Turn the abundance of summer into an instantly nutritious and invigorating drink.

Makes 1 serving, 8 ounces

Extract juice from vegetables, alternating leafy greens, herbs and onions with the tomatoes and carrot. Stir and season with salt.

ZIPPY GREEN AND GREEN

3 stalks celery, cut crosswise
into 1-inch pieces
1 cucumber, peeled and cut
into pieces to fit feed tube
½ jalapeño pepper, seeds
removed
Dash of seasoning salt

Cucumbers are one of nature's best diuretics and kidney cleansers. They are available year round. Especially delicious is the hothouse or English variety that comes wrapped in clear plastic. Cucumbers are an excellent source of juice and blend well with the celery in this recipe to give you a potassium and magnesium boost. Roasting the jalapeño slightly gives a subtle smokey flavor to this juice. It's an excellent lunch or mid-morning drink to take to work.

Makes 1 serving, 6 to 8 ounces, depending on size of cucumber

Extract juice from celery, cucumber and jalapeño pepper. Stir and season to taste.

THE GREEN GODDESS

½ English cucumber
2 green onions, cut crosswise
in 1-inch pieces
8 to 10 sprigs watercress
4 sprigs fresh dill
Dash of salt
1 tablespoon lemon juice

The English cucumber is a relatively new arrival in our markets, and well worth trying. Grown in greenhouses, it has no seeds and is dependably delicious. My first contact with English cucumbers was in a restaurant kitchen where an inspired Chinese cook used them daily. They were sweet and firm when sautéed with butter and dill. We used them in soups and of course in salads. Because the skin is softer than that of other varieties, they do not require peeling and have a much better yield. This helps to offset their slightly higher price.

This Green Goddess recipe is really an instant salad in a glass. It is fresh, flavorful, completely digestible, and easy to make. The addition of watercress gives your drink a spicy lift while dill and lemon give it an instant dressing.

Makes 1 serving, 6 ounces

Extract juice from vegetables, processing onions, watercress and dill along with cucumber pieces. Stir extracted juice and season with salt and lemon juice.

SMOKEY JOE

2 medium tomatoes
2 tomatillos
1 orange, rind removed
1 handful cilantro leaves
½ chipolte pepper*
Dash of salt (optional)

*Any leftover peppers can be stored in the refrigerator or frozen. Use them to flavor dips or pasta sauces.

There is no substitute for chipotle chiles, which are actually jalapeños that have been dried and smoked. The undeniable smokey flavor is what gives Joe his name. This drink would go well with a Sunday brunch of huevos rancheros, a Monday Night Football gathering with dips and salsas, or a Texas-style barbecue with beans. Smokey Joe will give you a surprising sizzle.

Makes 1 serving, 6 ounces

Feed all ingredients into feed tube and extract juice. Add a dash of salt if desired.

LA PROVENCE

3 tomatoes, cut to fit feed tube
2 cloves roasted garlic, (see below)
Few sprigs of Italian parsley
Few sprigs of tarragon
Dash of salt (optional)

Redolent of herbs and garlic, the sunny region of Provence inspires some of my favorite dishes. This Provençal version of tomato juice uses the savory flavor of roasted garlic with fresh tomatoes and fragrant tarragon. Enjoy this as a luncheon or appetizer juice.

Makes 1 serving, 8 ounces

Extract juice from tomato pieces alternately with garlic, parsley and tarragon. Stir. Season with salt if desired.

ROASTED GARLIC

1 head garlic
Olive oil for brushing

Cut across top of garlic head to expose cloves. Brush with olive oil. Wrap in foil and bake in oven for 30 minutes.

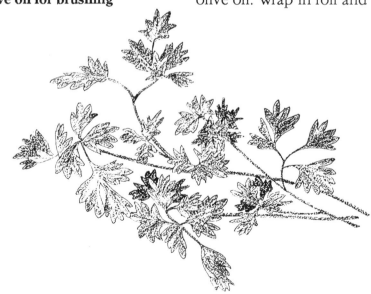

GINGER JUICE

The Chinese were using ginger in the sixth century BC to enliven their cuisine. It travelled with Arab traders into the Mediterranean region, then on to Spain and the West Indies by the sixteenth century. Ginger has found a home in contemporary dishes ranging from stir fry to apple pie. In fact, most westerners associate ginger with sweets such as gingerbread and ice cream. The delicate, piquant flavor of this gnarly brown root is our objective in using it extensively for drinks, dressings, dips and marinades.

Keep a few frozen cubes of ginger juice on hand for a great sense of security when unexpected company comes and you want to whip up a quick dip or dessert. For a fast dinner, thaw some frozen prawns and make a ginger marinade while the grill gets hot. Ginger is very popular in combination with carrots, and we love it in our Carrot Ginger Splash (page 32). Wait till you taste the ginger and lime sauce over fresh strawberries in Strawberries Yin Yang (page 109). Try ginger in your own juice combinations and you'll grow to love it too.

To juice ginger, prepare by peeling the ginger and slicing it crosswise in ⅛-inch slices. Place in feed tube and extract juice. Use immediately or freeze in ice cube trays.

CARROT GINGER SPLASH

2 large carrots, cut into pieces
1 orange, rind and seeds
removed
1 or 2 teaspoons ginger juice,
or 2 thin slices of fresh
ginger

Ginger has long been a staple in Asian kitchens. Combinations of vegetables and ginger are becoming more familiar as we sample the sweetness of carrots with the fresh hot taste of ginger, as in this recipe. By adding the juice of an orange, you can have a refreshing and vitamin-packed drink that's easy to take along in a lunch or picnic thermos.

Makes 1 serving, 8 ounces

Extract juice from carrots, orange and fresh ginger, if using fresh ginger, or combine extracted carrot/orange juice with prepared ginger juice. Chill and serve.

To make a spritzer, add sparkling soda or seltzer water. Serve over ice.

PURE GOLD

½ pineapple, peeled, cored,
cut to fit feed tube
½ large carrot, cut to fit feed
tube
1 orange, peeled and sec-
tioned, or ¼ cup reamed
orange juice
1 teaspoon ginger juice
(optional)

Strike it rich in vitamins A and C as you treat yourself to Pure Gold. Enjoy the drink immediately after juicing for maximum nutritional benefit. For a flavor change add a dash of ginger juice or a splash of seltzer water.

Makes 1 serving, 6 to 7 ounces

Extract juice from fruit. Add orange juice (extracted or reamed), and ginger juice if desired. Stir and serve.

THE UNDERGROUND

1 beet, cut to fit feed tube
2 large carrots, cut to fit feed tube
Sprigs of parsley or spinach leaves (optional)

These days rutabagas, parsnips and turnips have taken a back seat to carrots and beets. Carrots contain a healthy dose of vitamins A and E while beets supply potassium and iron. Both vegetables are a source of energy without fat, and yield abundant juice. You may find the juice from carrots and beets overly sweet, so we recommend adding a bit of parsley or spinach. Enjoy this drink while it's fresh to gain the full nutritional benefit.

Makes 1 serving, 8 ounces

Extract juice from beet and carrots. Stir and serve. If you choose to add parsley or spinach, process along with the beet and carrots.

A HOT TAMALE

Kernels from 2 ears of corn
2 large tomatoes, cut to fit feed tube
½ jalapeño pepper or a few drops hot-pepper sauce
Dash of salt (optional)

Tamale pie is a favorite of mine. Fresh corn, tomatoes and chiles crowd produce stands in summer, or perhaps they grow alongside each other in your own garden. This drink is quicker to make than homemade tamales and has the satisfying flavor of that favorite food.

Makes 1 serving, 6 ounces

Extract juice from corn and tomatoes. Season by processing jalapeño with the corn and tomatoes, or add a few drops of hot-pepper sauce. Season with salt if desired.

CUCUMBER BUTTERMILK FLIP

1 small cucumber or
  ½ English cucumber
½ lemon, rind removed
8 sprigs dill
8 sprigs watercress
½ cup buttermilk
Dash of salt or celery salt
  (optional)

This is an immensely refreshing drink for sipping on an outdoor patio some sunny afternoon. Reminiscent of soups made with yogurt and cucumbers, it has a brisk buttermilk flavor combined with the lightness of lemon and dill. We recommend the English cucumbers because of their consistently sweet juicy quality. Watercress is a green herb that will enhance your flip with zip.

Makes 2 servings, 6 ounces each

Extract juice, processing dill and watercress along with the cucumber and lemon. Combine with buttermilk and salt if desired. Whip with immersion blender if desired.

BORSCHT COCKTAIL

¼ cup beet juice
2 tablespoons carrot juice
1 tablespoon lemon juice
¼ cup yogurt or buttermilk
½ teaspoon horseradish
½ teaspoon ginger juice,
  optional
Minced fresh dill, for garnish

Beets are now commonplace in our markets. They are probably best in the spring and summer, with the small green leaves attached to prove they've just been thinned from a larger patch. Varieties of golden beets are just as sweet as the red and would add another beautiful hue to this cocktail. Because both carrots and beets are root vegetables, a Borscht Cocktail does your body a great favor by providing high levels of potassium, loads of vitamin A and completely fat-free energy. As the French say, *A votre santé,* "To your health."

Makes 1 serving, 6 ounces

Combine juices, yogurt or buttermilk, horseradish and ginger juice, if used, in blender, or whip with an immersion blender. Pour into serving glass and garnish with dill.

SPECIAL JUICE DRINKS

Aguas Frescas and Liquados

Mexico is famous for a variety of drinks ranging from tequila to cocoa. Many of the fruit drinks are made by fermenting local fruits such as pineapples, grapes and berries. Some areas use locally grown sugar cane juice for sweetener and other areas use mineral waters from neighboring springs to add a regional touch. Often served from vendor carts in the town streets as well as at restaurants and in market places, aguas frescas and liquados are very popular in Mexico.

One of two prep cooks in our catering company from Mexico, Juan, says that in his region of Michoacan, aguas frescas are a combination of fresh fruit, crushed ice, water and sugar. Liquados combine fresh fruit, crushed ice, milk and sugar. Experiment with fruit combinations that sound good to you. These recipes are based on some of Juan's favorites.

If you do not want to use sugar, try the drinks with sugar omitted, or add 2 tablespoons of extracted white grape juice.

Aguas Frescas

Each recipe makes two 6-ounce servings.

PINEAPPLE AGUA FRESCA

1 fresh pineapple, peeled and cored
1 cup crushed ice
1 cup water
1 tablespoon superfine sugar

STRAWBERRY PEACH AGUA FRESCA

1 pint strawberries, hulled
1 peach, pit removed
1 cup crushed ice
½ cup water
1 tablespoon superfine sugar

MANGO AGUA FRESCA

3 mangos, pits removed
½ cup water
1 cup crushed ice
1 tablespoon superfine sugar

KUMQUAT AGUA FRESCA

1½ cups kumquats
½ cup water
1 cup crushed ice
2 tablespoons superfine sugar

WATERMELON AGUA FRESCA

½ medium watermelon, rind and seeds
  removed
1 cup crushed ice
1 tablespoon superfine sugar

For drink selected, extract juice from fruit. Combine remaining ingredients in blender and blend for 20 seconds. Strain mixture into tall glasses.

TAMARIND AGUA FRESCA

**2 cups frozen tamarindade
   cubes (page 39)
1 tablespoons superfine
   sugar
¼ cup orange juice**

Makes 4 servings, 5 ounces each

Allow tamarindade cubes to melt slightly. Combine tamarindade cubes, sugar and orange juice. Blend until smooth. Serve over ice.

Liquados

Each recipe makes two 6-ounce servings.

STRAWBERRY LIQUADO

**1 pint strawberries, hulled
1 tablespoon superfine sugar
¼ cup milk
½ cup crushed ice**

PINEAPPLE LIQUADO

**1 pineapple, rind and core removed
½ cup milk
1 tablespoon superfine sugar
½ cup crushed ice**

PEACH LIQUADO

**3 peaches, pits removed
1 tablespoon superfine sugar
¼ cup milk
½ cup crushed ice**

Extract juice from fruit. Combine with sugar, milk and crushed ice. Blend until smooth. About 30 seconds.

GLACÉS

Most aguas frescas become glacés by substituting fruit syrups for the sugar. Fine-quality fruit syrups such as boysenberry, peach and apricot would make delicious glacés. The Pink Flamingo was a stand-out at a Macy's juice bar I happened into one Saturday. When pomegranates are in season, you can make this drink and sweeten it with extracted grape juice. When pomegranates are out of season, substitute one or two tablespoons grenadine for the pomegranate seeds and grapes, and omit additional sweetener.

PINK FLAMINGO GLACÉ

1 pomegranate, seeds only
½ pineapple, shell and core
**   removed**
1 papaya, peeled and seeds
**   removed**
½ cup grapes, stems removed
1 cup crushed ice

Makes 1 serving

Extract juice from pomegranate, pineapple, papaya and grapes. Combine with ice in blender and blend until smooth.

TAMARINDADE

20 tamarind pods
1 cup sugar
6 cups warm water
Sugar to taste

A common sight in the landscape of India is the handsome tamarind tree. Fruit from the tree consists of large, bean-shaped pods that produce a liquid used much the way lemon or vinegar is used in Western cuisines. Tamarind, greatly valued in the cuisines of the East and even the West Indies for its refreshing, cooling qualities, is used in curries, chutneys, jams and jellies. The juice can be preserved in syrup or as paste, or combined with water and sugar to create a zesty, delicious drink reminiscent of lemonade. I like my tamarindade on the tart side.

I recommend freezing tamarindade in ice cube trays for use in fruit juice drinks and teas that need a lively kick. Add it to tropical fruit drinks to create a scrumptious Carribbean "sky juice." You can buy tamarindo concentrate in the juice section of many Latin American markets, but it will lack the pure flavor of this home brew.

Remove the long thin outer shell of tamarind pods. Combine pods and 1 cup sugar in warm water and let soak 1 hour. Strain, saving the liquid. With a wooden spoon or pestle, push pulp through strainer. Discard the hard seeds and membranes left in the sieve. Combine the strained liquid with the pulp and mix well. Sweeten with sugar to taste.

Iced Teas, Citrus Coolers and Spritzers

It wasn't too many years ago when a restaurant or market offering herbal teas was considered quite trendy. Luckily, the makers of teas heard our plea and have supplied us with an array of herbal brews for every taste. With fresh juices to enhance the flavors in teas, you can create a new drink entirely. Whether you choose the decaffeinated varieties or some of the traditional Asian and orange pekoe teas, these juice and tea combinations served over ice with mint or lemon slices will leave you feeling refreshed.

Lemonade has always brought back fond memories of my childhood days and large pitchers of freshly squeezed lemonade. My dad was a little ahead of his time, it seems, when he made his specialty of lemonade and seltzer water: a lemonade spritzer. Any citrus juice can be combined with a little sweetener, diluted with water and served over ice. Call them citrus coolers and use grapefruit, limes, tangerines and oranges. Keep going and add soda water or sparkling mineral water and you have a spritzer. Bottled mineral waters with juice and flavorings abound in today's markets, but you can make your own with the flavors you prefer.

LEMON STRAWBERRY CHAMOMILE TEA

1 lemon herb tea bag
1 chamomile tea bag
½ cup strawberry juice
½ cup red grape juice
1 tablespoon honey
   (optional)

Whenever I have chamomile tea or make a cup for one of my children, I think of poor Peter Rabbit and his misadventure in Mr. McGregor's garden. Chamomile flowers are known for their medicinal benefits in settling a stomach ache or breaking a fever. I even had a chamomile steam facial that was a heavenly cleansing for my skin. The best part of the facial was being enveloped in the aroma of apples and melons that chamomile flowers exude.

If you haven't experimented with iced herb teas, you have a wonderful treat ahead. This tea will delight you with its fragrance and succulent flavors. It makes an excellent picnic drink to take in a cooler or a refreshing way to end a morning of gardening. Treat yourself!

Makes 4 servings, 6 ounces each

Brew tea with 2 cups hot water. Allow to cool.

Combine tea with strawberry and red grape juice. Add honey if desired. Chill and serve over ice.

JAMAICA FLOWER TEA DRINKS

Most Latin American markets offer booths with large displays of dried hibiscus flowers. The flowers can be steeped in boiling water to make a dark red aromatic tea. If you were in the Caribbean, the same red drink would be made from sorrel flowers, a member of the hibiscus family. Island teas are mixed with rum, ginger, lemon zest and cloves to make a festive Christmas drink. This version combines hibiscus flower tea with fresh strawberries and mint for a tart but refreshing cooler.

Making this tea is a perfect opportunity to use your frozen juice cubes of pineapple, tamarindade, strawberry, raspberry or ginger. The flavors swirl and enhance the tea as the cubes melt. Depending on the sweetness of the juices, you may wish to add simple syrup or sugar.

JAMAICA FLOWER TEA

Use four to six dried hibiscus flowers to make one cup of tea. In teapot or crock, place flowers, cover with boiling water and let steep 10 minutes. Pour tea through strainer and into teacup.

STRAWBERRY JAMAICA FLOWER TEA

½ cup strawberry juice
(10 strawberries)
1 cup Jamaica Flower Tea
1 or 2 tablespoons simple
syrup (page 43)
Mint leaves as garnish

Makes 2 servings, 6 ounces each

Extract juice from strawberries. Combine with tea and simple syrup. Serve over ice and garnish with mint.

PINEAPPLE JAMAICA FLOWER TEA

½ cup pineapple juice
    (¼ pineapple, peeled and
    cored)
¼ cup apple juice (1 large
    apple)
½ cup Jamaica Flower Tea
Mint leaves, for garnish

Makes 1 serving, 6 ounces

Extract juice from pineapple and apple. Combine with tea. Serve over ice and garnish with mint.

TANGERINE JAMAICA FLOWER TEA

½ cup tangerine juice (2 to 3
    tangerines)
1 tablespoon simple syrup
    (see below)
½ cup Jamaica Flower Tea
Mint leaves, for garnish

Makes 1 serving, 5 ounces

Extract juice from tangerines. Combine with syrup and tea. Serve over ice and garnish with mint.

SIMPLE SYRUP

1 cup sugar
¾ cup water

Makes 1 ¾ cups.

Combine in saucepan and bring to a boil. Reduce heat and simmer for 3 minutes. Store covered in the refrigerator.

PINEAPPLE JAMAICA TAMARIND TEA

¼ cup pineapple juice
2 tablespoons apple juice
¼ cup Jamaica Flower Tea
   (page 42)
Frozen Tamarindade cubes
   (page 39)

Here is a tea to change your destiny. It's especially good when winter has had you indoors for months and your fireside reveries continually take you to a sunny island beach. If it's a steamy city summer and that same beach is beckoning, take off your shoes and sip Pineapple Jamaica Tea. This tea is a gentle sea breeze, an exotic barefoot romp and a great accompaniment to the Travel section of the Sunday paper. The tamarindade ice cubes give it a zing that's better than lemonade to take you far away.

Makes 1 serving, 5 ounces

Combine pineapple juice, apple juice and Jamaica Flower Tea. Pour over 2 or 3 tamarindade cubes.

LEMON MINT SPRITZER

½ cup sugar
½ cup water
1 tablespoon finely grated lemon rind
¼ cup fresh lemon juice
½ cup fresh mint leaves, washed and chopped
2 bottles (32 oz each) lemon-lime soda
Lemon slices and mint leaves, for garnish

This popular recipe from my *Teatime Celebrations* book came from childhood memories of walking down country roads with my two Scotty dogs, surrounded by blackberry bushes and peonies. My mother made lemon mint syrup and I turned it into this spritzer. You can double or triple the recipe of the lemon mint syrup to use as flavoring in iced tea or a light marinade for fresh fruit.

Makes 6 servings

In saucepan, combine sugar, water and lemon rind. Boil for several minutes. Remove from heat and stir in lemon juice. Bruise or chop mint to release juice, then add to saucepan and stir. Let mixture sit for several hours. Strain.

To make spritzer, fill tall glasses with ice. Add 2 to 3 tablespoons lemon syrup per glass and fill with soda. Garnish with lemon slice and fresh mint leaves.

KIWI SPRITZER

½ cup kiwi juice (approximately 2 kiwis, peeled)
2 tablespoons orange juice
1 tablespoon simple syrup (page 43)
10 ounces seltzer water or soda water

Kiwi fruit is imported from New Zealand, and Freda's Specialty Produce in Los Angeles is credited with the initial distribution here in the U.S. Kiwi is now being successfully grown in California, which should help make them more available. Kiwis are tart like citrus and have dazzling eye-appeal. They could have been designed to be served in a fruit bowl. This recipe takes advantage of kiwi's brisk, flavorful juice.

Makes 2 servings, 8 ounces each

Extract kiwi juice. Add orange juice and simple syrup. Pour over ice into 2 glasses. Add seltzer water and stir well.

GINGER PINEAPPLE KIWI SPRITZER

**2 tablespoons pineapple juice
(¼ pineapple)
2 tablespoons kiwi juice
(1 kiwi)
2 slices ginger
1 teaspoon simple syrup
Soda or seltzer water
Mint sprig, for garnish**

Ginger as part of a spritzer definitely adds "spritz" to the flavor. I find this spritzer a refreshing summertime drink. Serve it with a sprig of mint for garnish.

Makes 1 serving, 8 ounces

Extract juice from fruit, processing ginger at the same time. Add simple syrup; stir and pour into glass. Add soda water and garnish with mint.

STRAWBERRY SPRITZER

**¾ cup strawberry juice
(1 pint berries)
¼ cup grape juice (½ cup
grapes, stems removed)
1 teaspoon ginger juice
(page 31)
Gingerale or lemon-lime soda**

A myriad of spritzers can be made using fresh fruit juices and gingerale or lemon-lime soda for the final spritz. I like to add a little mint or ginger juice for additional flavoring. Experiment with other berry juices, or substitute peach or nectarine juice for more fresh fruit spritzers.

Makes 1 serving, 8 ounces

Combine strawberry, grape and ginger juice. Divide among 4 goblets. Add small amount of crushed ice and fill glasses with gingerale or lemon-lime soda. Stir.

HERBAL FRUIT SYRUPS

Most markets these days offer a selection of seasonal fresh herbs that have become familiar to us. Basil, cilantro, chives, mint and dill appear in lovely little bunches that can inspire a cooking adventure or a beautiful garnish. I'm lucky to live near Quail Mountain Herbs, a company large enough to market herbs worldwide and still meet my unusual requests as I develop recipes. These herbal syrups can be used as a base for spritzers, flavorings for iced tea or as marinades for fresh fruit.

ORANGE BASIL

½ cup sugar
½ cup water
Zest of 1 orange
⅓ cup orange juice
1 tablespoon lemon juice
2 tablespoons chopped basil

PINEAPPLE ROSEMARY

½ cup sugar
½ cup water
Zest of 1 lemon
⅓ cup pineapple juice
1 tablespoon lemon juice
2 or 3 sprigs rosemary

Makes 1⅓ cups

In saucepan, combine sugar, water and zest. Bring to a boil and cook for 2 to 3 minutes. Remove from heat and stir in juice. Allow to cool slightly; stir in herbs. Let sit for 2 hours. Strain and chill.

Recipe can be doubled or tripled and kept refrigerated.

Smoothies

Smoothies are the inevitable product of kids and blenders. With a simple piece of equipment and one or two favorite foods, you can create a healthful, satisfying repast. Ingredients should be limited to two or three at the most, so flavors are distinct. I use bananas to sweeten and thicken the drink, and nonfat milk to avoid the fats of dairy products. The advantage of using extracted juice is that there are no seeds. The ripest fruit and spotted bananas are perfect for smoothies. In minutes, you can have an excellent liquid lunch or a rejuvenator for active people, young and not-so-young.

STRAWBERRY BANANA SMOOTHIE

6 ounces strawberry juice
(1 pint fresh berries)
1 ripe banana, peeled and cut
in pieces
3 tablespoons powdered non-
fat milk
½ cup crushed ice
1 or 2 tablespoons protein
powder (optional)

Makes 2 servings, 5 ounces each

Blend all ingredients in blender or whip with an immersion blender.

ORANGE PRUNE SMOOTHIE

¼ cup orange juice
2 tablespoons carrot juice
6 pitted prunes
2 tablespoons powdered non-
fat milk
½ cup crushed ice

Makes 1 serving, 5 ounces

Combine orange juice, carrot juice, prunes, milk and crushed ice in blender, or whip with an immersion blender. If consistency is too thick, add 2 tablespoons of water, carrot juice or more orange juice.

PINEAPPLE SMOOTHIE

1 cup pineapple juice (about
½ pineapple, rind and core
removed)
1 ripe banana peeled, and cut
in pieces
3 tablespoons powdered non-
fat milk
½ cup crushed ice
1 tablespoon protein powder
(optional)

Makes 2 servings, 5 ounces each

Blend all ingredients in blender or whip with an immersion blender.

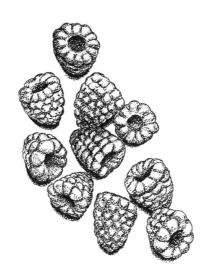

MANGO MELBA SMOOTHIE

1 cup mango purée (about
    3 mangos, pits removed)
½ cup raspberry nectar
    (½ pint fresh berries)
1 ripe banana peeled, and cut
    in pieces
3 tablespoons powdered non-
    fat milk
½ cup crushed ice

Makes 2 servings, 6 ounces each

Blend all ingredients in blender or whip with an immersion blender.

SUMMER MEDLEY SMOOTHIE

¼ cup peach nectar
¼ cup apricot nectar
¼ cup plum nectar
1 tablespoon honey
1 ripe banana peeled, and cut
    in pieces
½ cup crushed ice
2 tablespoons powdered non-
    fat milk

Makes 2 servings, 5 ounces each

Blend all ingredients in blender or whip with an immersion blender.

PURPLE COW

½ cup blueberry juice
2 tablespoons orange juice
⅓ ripe banana, peeled and
  cut in pieces
2 tablespoons powdered non-
  fat milk
Seltzer water or club soda to
  taste

Whether your blueberries are grown in Maine or Oregon, this recipe makes a rich-tasting, beautiful blue shake. When I lived with my aunt in New York, she made "black cows" or root beer floats. Here is a low calorie "cow" made with non-fat milk. It's a great morning starter drink or an after-school treat in a soda-fountain-style glass.

Makes 1 serving, 6 ounces

Combine blueberry juice, orange juice, banana and powdered milk in blender, or whip with immersion blender. Divide between two glasses. Add seltzer water or club soda to taste, and stir.

PEACHES 'N' CREAM

½ cup peach nectar (2 large
  peaches)
⅔ cup buttermilk
2 teaspoons sugar
¼ teaspoon ground cin-
  namon

This recipe reminds me of a favorite dessert my mother made from cream cheese, buttermilk, cinnamon and peaches. The peaches released their juice as the dessert baked, so by the time it was chilled for serving the flavors were richly blended.

It makes a marvelous brunch or luncheon drink. But try it for breakfast sometime too, in place of those buttermilk pancakes you don't have time to make.

Makes 2 servings, 5 ounces each

Combine peach juice, buttermilk, sugar and cinnamon with whisk, or blend in blender or with an immersion blender.

BLUEBERRIES 'N' CREAM

⅔ cup blueberry juice (1 pint
  fresh berries)
2 teaspoons lemon juice
2 tablespoons simple syrup
  (page 43) or 2 tablespoons
  sugar
⅓ cup half and half, or heavy
  cream

Tarts, pies, jams, soups and sauces made with blueberries often call for lemon peel or lemon juice to be included. The aromatic peel and tart, sharp taste of lemon offsets the sweet, flowery blueberry to perfection. This recipe is a yummy way to cool off an afternoon. It also makes a light but satisfying dessert drink.

Makes 2 servings, 10 ounces

Combine blueberry juice, lemon juice, syrup (or sugar) and half and half in blender, or whip with immersion blender.

VERY BERRY ROYALE

½ pint raspberries
½ pint blackberries
½ pint strawberries
1 bottle Champagne
Fresh berries, for garnish

We have a dear friend whose house is in the midst of a glorious apple orchard, along one side of which is a thicket of blackberry bushes at least four feet deep. Since blackberries are the scarcest of all the wild berries in our country, this thicket is a preciously guarded secret. In late summer when the apples are spending their last weeks getting juicy and rosy red, but are not yet ready for picking, we get into our combat boots, long sleeves and gloves to pick buckets of ripe sweet blackberries. We fuel ourselves through the hot afternoon by eating the very ripest and juiciest of the berries, lest they be crushed before we can get them home. The satisfaction of knowing our freezer will be stocked with bags of perfect berries and juice is consolation for the purple-stained fingertips and lips.

Blackberry juice can be combined with other fruits for a slightly tart flavor. It's wonderful with those luscious apples when they are finally ready to be picked. And, when the juice is combined with a bottle of Champagne, it becomes a memorable celebration.

Makes 4 servings

Combine berry juices and divide among 4 Champagne flutes. Add Champagne to fill glasses. Garnish with fresh berries. You may combine the juices as you are extracting each one. Continuously feed berries through the extractor, allowing juices to mix in receptacle. Stir a few times to combine.

RASPBERRY PUNCH

½ cup grape juice (about
   1 cup grapes, stems
   removed)
½ cup raspberry nectar
   (1 pint raspberries)
2 tablespoons lime juice
¼ cup raspberry liqueur or
   Cassis
2 bottles Champagne
1 prepared Frozen Juice Ring
   (page 55)

Here is that very special occasion punch you may want to keep mentally filed away for weddings, showers, summer gatherings and backyard croquet games. The sweetness comes from white grape juice, which you can increase depending on the amount of sweetness desired. I prefer punch to be fruity but on the tart side. You may vary the fresh fruits and liqueurs or use a combination.

Makes 12 servings

Combine grape juice, raspberry nectar and lime juice in small punch bowl. Chill. When ready to serve add raspberry liqueur and Champagne to punch base. Add Frozen Juice Ring.

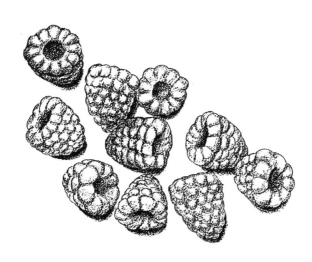

GINGER STRAWBERRY PINEAPPLE PUNCH

**1½ cups strawberry nectar
(about 3 pints)**
**8 slices peeled fresh ginger,
juice extracted**
**1 cup pineapple juice (about
1¼ pineapple)**
⅓ cup lemon juice
⅓ cup simple syrup (page 43)
2 quarts gingerale

Ginger has been valued for centuries for its medicinal bene-fit and as a culinary spice. Its pungent and aromatic bou-quet finds its way into a variety of foods, such as Asian crab, English gingerbread, and ginger mustard glaze for barbecues. Ginger has been used as a curative for the plague, in potpourris to freshen the air, and as a supposed aphrodisiac. With such a diverse history, ginger could add an interesting blast-off to your party punch. Use only fresh ginger in this recipe to avoid the musty sharp taste that powdered ginger can sometimes have.

When juicing large quantities of fruit, be sure to empty the receptacle frequently. A special solution for keeping the punch cold without diluting it is the Frozen Juice Ring (see below).

Makes 12 servings

Combine strawberry nectar, ginger, pineapple and lemon juices, and simple syrup. Chill. Pour punch base into punch bowl, add Frozen Juice Ring. Slowly pour in gingerale.

FROZEN JUICE RING

Extract juice from assorted fruits (peaches, nectarines, apri-cots, plums, berries). Pour in small decorative ring mold. Add ½ pint strawberries. Freeze.

A SPECIAL SANGRIA

½ cup plum juice
½ cup nectarine juice
½ cup mixed berry juice
   (raspberry, blackberry,
   strawberry)
¼ cup orange juice
2 tablespoons sugar, or to
   taste
1 750 ml bottle fruity red
   wine
Fresh fruit slices for garnish
   (3 apricots, 2 plums, 2
   nectarines, 1 orange)
¼ cup brandy (optional)

Served in an elegant glass pitcher with slices of fresh fruit for garnish, this sangria makes a beautiful presentation. The real delight is tasting very fresh fruit juices mixed with red wine. Sangria is a favorite summer cooler, great at outdoor parties.

Makes 4 servings, 6 ounces each

In a tall pitcher, combine fruit juices. Add sugar and combine well. Pour in wine and add sliced fruit and brandy, if desired. Chill well until ready to serve. Pour into stemmed wine glasses with a slice or two of fruit for garnish.

BEYOND JUICE

SOUPS

Making soup brings back childhood memories for me. My sisters and I were always in the kitchen baking or helping to prepare meals. We liked to bake fresh bread and make a meal of soup and bread. A simple freshly made soup will bring delight to your dining table too.

Your juice extractor makes it a breeze to prepare these soup recipes. On hot summer days enjoy the chilled soups, particularly the gazpachos. When it's cool and foggy a hot soup can be comforting. Serve soup as a first course or a main course, garnished with fresh fruit, vegetables or flowers. As you experiment with different types of juices and broths, remember to add some potato juice as a thickener. You'll be amazed at its power.

GINGER CARROT SQUASH BISQUE

1 cup carrot juice (3 large carrots)
1 cup chicken stock (recipe follows)
½ cup cooked yellow squash (acorn or butternut)
1 to 2 tablespoons ginger juice
1 cup half and half
¼ cup potato juice (½ potato)
Salt and white pepper to taste
Chopped chives or dill, as garnish

Bisque is a thick, creamy purée of vegetables that makes a hearty meal with salad and bread, or a rich first course to a formal meal. I've praised the combination of carrots and ginger many times as a sweet and piquant delicacy. The golden color of this soup adds a mellowness that reminds me of autumn. It's especially nice garnished with fresh dill or chives, or a bit of both.

Serves 4

Combine carrot juice, chicken broth and squash. Blend in blender until smooth.

In medium saucepan, combine blended mixture with ginger juice.

Combine half and half and potato juice and add to soup mixture. Heat just to boiling, then simmer until soup thickens, about 5 minutes. Stir frequently.

Season with salt and white pepper to taste. Garnish with chives or dill.

CHICKEN STOCK

5 pounds assorted chicken parts (necks, wings, backs)
2 leeks
1 large onion, quartered
2 large carrots
5 sprigs fresh parsley
2 stalks celery, including leaves
1 teaspoon salt

Makes 2 ½ quarts

In a large stock pot place chicken parts. Cover with 3 quarts cold water and bring to a boil; skim off scum from surface. Add leeks, onion, carrots, parsley, celery and salt. Simmer partially covered, about 1½ to 2 hours. Remove chicken. Strain stock through a colander or sieve lined with a double thickness of dampened cheesecloth. Refrigerate overnight. Remove hardened fat on the surface.

For extra-rich stock, boil and reduce stock to 1½ quarts.

CREAM OF ROASTED RED BELL PEPPER

1 cup carrot or tomato juice
   (3 large)
1 cup roasted red bell pepper
   juice (4 large)
¼ cup cup potato juice
   (½ potato)
1 cup milk or half and half
½ teaspoon salt
Pepper to taste
1 tablespoon fresh marjoram
   or thyme or 1 teaspoon
   crushed dried herb

Roasted bell peppers add a depth of smokey flavor to this cream soup. The thickening ingredient is the potato starch in the potato juice. For additional texture, ½ cup cooked rice or barley may be added.

Serves 4

Combine carrot or tomato juice, roasted red bell pepper juice and salt. Heat to simmering.

Combine potato juice and milk or half and half. Add to soup mixture along with salt and cook, stirring frequently, until soup thickens.

Season with additional salt if desired and pepper.

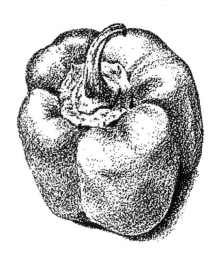

CREAM OF TOMATO BASIL SOUP

**2 cups fresh tomato juice
(6 to 7 tomatoes)
¼ cup leek juice (2 large
leeks)
¼ cup potato juice (½ potato)
1 cup milk or half and half
Salt and pepper to taste
Chiffonade of basil leaves, for
garnish**

When shiny green basil leaves meet a juicy fresh tomato, it's an Italian love match. The sweet-scented perfume of basil compliments a ripe, juicy tomato to perfection. In my garden, I can almost catch the two growing nearer as they get tall and bushy. Most of us plant much more than we can consume in one season, so the basil becomes a supply of pesto and the tomatoes become juice and purée to use all winter long. This soup is a savory celebration of a classic combination. Enjoy it for a late summer supper or a lunch some wintry day.

Serves 4

Heat tomato and leek juice. Combine potato juice with milk or half and half, and add to juice mixture.

Cook soup, stirring frequently until thickened. Season with salt and pepper. Garnish with chiffonade of basil leaves.

To make the chiffonade, stack several basil leaves, then cut crosswise in very thin slices. Use a sharp knife.

AVOCADO GAZPACHO

1 quart tomato juice (12 to 14
  tomatoes)
½ cup canned tomato purée
3 medium avocados, peeled
  and cubed
1 medium cucumber, peeled
  and chopped
1 large green pepper, cored,
  seeded and chopped
2 large tomatoes, chopped
4 to 5 green onions, finely
  chopped
2 tablespoons minced fresh
  parsley
1 clove garlic, minced
2 tablespoons fresh lemon or
  lime juice
½ teaspoon hot-pepper sauce
½ teaspoon salt
⅛ teaspoon white pepper
1 cup croutons, for garnish

Recently we had a severe and unexpected freeze in the Pajaro Valley just when our two trusty avocado trees were loaded with baby avocados. The leaves and fruit froze, reducing our trees to life-sized stick drawings. A rainy March was followed by the warm days of April and May, bringing back to our trees leaf buds and later, new green growth. It may still be a few years before we have avocados, but we're grateful the trees were not lost, and we'll make this a family lesson in patience. When the tomato season bestows on us its bounty of juicy, ripe tomatoes, serve this gazpacho, adding avocado for the special nutty flavor it provides.

Serves 8

In a large bowl, combine all ingredients except croutons. Chill thoroughly for 2 to 3 hours.

Serve in chilled bowls. Garnish with croutons.

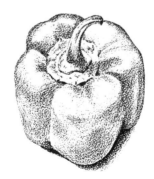

WATERMELON GAZPACHO

2½ cups watermelon juice
(about ½ melon)
2 tomatoes, peeled, seeded
and chopped
1 cucumber, peeled and diced
3 green onions, minced
(some of the green tops
included)
½ cup croutons, for garnish

More than a soup, gazpacho is fresh vegetables to sip and crunch. It's full of onion, cucumber and sometimes pepper bits to nibble while you sip a cup of cold, nutritious juice. Gazpacho makes an excellent light lunch, a fact well known by calorie counters. If you like your gazpacho a bit thicker, process the watermelon juice in a blender with half a banana.

Serves 4

Place watermelon juice in soup tureen. Add tomatoes, cucumber and green onions. Stir to combine.

ASIAN GAZPACHO

3 cups chicken stock
1 stalk lemon grass, trimmed
    and cut crosswise into
    ½-inch pieces
1 cup shredded daikon radish
¼ cup celery juice (1 stalk
    celery)
1 cup chopped cucumber
⅓ cup thinly sliced green
    onions
½ cup diced red bell pepper
½ cup diced yellow bell
    pepper
1 tablespoon bottled fish
    sauce (nam pla)
1 teaspoon sesame oil
2 tablespoons lime juice
½ cup enoki mushrooms, for
    garnish
⅓ cup cilantro leaves, for
    garnish

Asian cuisine has made an irrevocable entrance into the western world. As a result, we have discovered textures of unusual mushrooms, the pungency of ginger, the nutty flavor of toasted sesame seeds, and the art of precisely cut and cooked vegetables. This gazpacho celebrates the flavors of the Orient. Any Asian market will carry the ingredients called for, and some large supermarkets are beginning to carry both fresh Asian ingredients as well as a selection of sauces.

Serves 6

Heat chicken stock and lemon grass together until lemon grass is tender. Stir in radish. Chill.

Add celery juice, cucumber, green onion, red and yellow bell pepper, fish sauce, sesame oil and lime juice. Chill several hours.

Ladle into soup bowls and garnish with mushrooms and cilantro.

PINEAPPLE PEACH SOUP

**2½ cups pineapple juice
(3 pineapples)
3 tablespoons quick-cooking
tapioca
Sprig of rosemary
2 peaches, peeled and diced**

Now that pineapples are available to us year round in most areas, this soup can be a tropical escape on a hot summer afternoon or a refreshing starter at brunch. Fruit soups are very popular in Scandinavian countries, where they are served both warm and chilled. We like this one nicely chilled.

Serves 4

Combine 1 cup pineapple juice and tapioca in medium saucepan. Allow to set for about 5 minutes. Bring to a boil and cook until thickened, about 5 minutes.

Remove from heat. Add sprig of rosemary. Cover and allow to cool. Add remaining pineapple juice and chill.

When ready to serve, add prepared peaches and serve in chilled bowls.

STRAWBERRY GINGER SOUP WITH BERRIES

**2¼ cups strawberry juice
(3 pints strawberries)
1 to 2 tablespoons ginger
juice
1 banana
½ cup raspberries
½ cup blueberries or blackberries**

Fresh ginger adds a very subtle flavor to this chilled soup. Use the berries fresh from your roadside stand or farmer's market and your soup will change with the summer's bounty.

Serve 4

Combine strawberry juice, ginger juice and banana in blender; blend until smooth.

Place mixture in attractive serving bowl or soup tureen. Add berries and stir to combine.

MELON SOUP WITH STRAWBERRIES

1 pint strawberries, washed and hulled
4 medium cantaloupes, rind and seeds removed
2 cups Muscat Canelli wine
1 cup fresh orange juice
1 cup pineapple juice or papaya nectar
⅓ cup fresh lime juice
1 bottle Champagne or 1 quart lemon-lime soda

This recipe is a longtime favorite from my first cookbook, *Kitchen Tools: Cooking With A Twist and A Flair*. I've included this soup here because of the many fresh fruit juices it uses. Try it for a special Sunday brunch and it may become a classic for you too.

Serves 10 to 12

Halve large strawberries, chill.

With melon baller, cut balls from one of the cantaloupes and chill. Cut remaining 3 melons into chunks. Place chunks and any cantaloupe remaining after making balls into a food processor. Process until smooth. If using a blender, process in 3 small batches, adding some pineapple juice with each batch.

In a chilled soup tureen, place cantaloupe purée, wine, orange, pineapple and lime juices. (The soup can be made ahead of time to this point and refrigerated.)

To serve, add Champagne or lemon-lime soda and stir. Add strawberries and melon balls.

QUICK BORSCHT

1 cup beef broth
¾ cup beet juice (about
    3 beets)
½ cup carrot juice (1½ large
    carrots)
2 tablespoons leek juice
    (2 leeks)
1½ cups shredded cabbage
1 tablespoon lemon juice
¼ to ½ teaspoon celery salt or
    celery-based seasoning
    blend
2 teaspoons horseradish
Sour cream, for garnish

This recipe can be served hot or cold. It's an easy way to combine the nutrients of beets and a refreshing soup in a simply styled borscht. When serving the soup cold, garnish with chopped dill or chives. For hot or cold borscht, add a generous dollop of sour cream.

Serves 4

In stainless steel saucepan combine beef broth with beet, carrot, and leek juice. Heat to boiling. Add cabbage and cook for two minutes.

Remove from heat and add lemon juice, celery salt to taste and horseradish. Stir to blend.

Ladle soup into bowls and garnish with sour cream.

CHILLED CUCUMBER SOUP WITH SHRIMP AND DILL

1 English cucumber (reserve
    ⅓ for making cucumber
    crescents)
1 lemon, rind removed
2 scallions, cut crosswise into
    ½-inch pieces
½ ripe banana
2 teaspoons minced fresh dill
½ jalapeño pepper, seeds
    removed
Dash of salt
¼ pound bay shrimp
Dill sprigs, for garnish

Cucumber soup is usually served on summer evenings to cool the palate after a long day. This is a refreshingly light lunch as well. A little jalapeño pepper makes this soup come alive and the added shrimp turns it into a meal.

Serves 2

Extract juice from cucumber, lemon and scallions. In blender, combine extracted juice, banana, dill, jalapeño and salt. Blend until smooth and chill.

Divide soup between two soup bowls. Add shrimp and cucumber crescents to each bowl and garnish with dill sprigs.

Cucumber crescents: Cut reserved cucumber piece in half lengthwise. Scoop seeds from center and cut crosswise into crescent pieces.

TOMATO CLAM CHOWDER

1 tablespoon butter or margarine
½ cup sliced leeks or onion
1½ potatoes, peeled and diced
1 bottle (8 oz) clam juice
2 tablespoons carrot juice (½ medium carrot)
1 cup tomato juice (3 large tomatoes)
¼ cup potato juice (½ potato)
Kernels from 2 ears of corn
½ teaspoon fines herbes, crushed
1 can (6 oz) clams, juice reserved
Salt and pepper to taste

When summer starts to disappear into fall and the days are upon us when kitchens light up earlier and people drift indoors with a chill—these spell "soup." My favorite two chowders are combined here, making this an uncontested winner on one of those chowder days. Use fresh tomatoes, carrots and corn for a special meal.

Serves 4

In medium saucepan, melt butter. Sauté leeks or onion until soft. Add diced potatoes and clam juice. Cook until potatoes are tender.

Stir in carrot, tomato and potato juices, corn kernels and fines herbes. Cook until thickened. Add drained clams. Season with salt and pepper to taste.

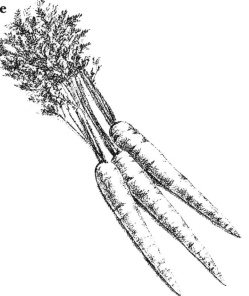

SALADS AND SALAD DRESSING

Salads may present you with some of the most creative uses yet of your juice extractor. By nature, salads call for crisp ingredients, colorful arrangements and delicate dressings. With the bounty of produce and aromatic herbs available to us seasonally, salads can be varied and exciting. Purées used as the main component in a dressing will keep calories and oil under control. You can enhance the purées with mint, cilantro, basil, or chervil and partner them with lettuces, vegetables, exotic fruits and savory legumes.

Festive presentations for aspics make them perfect for buffet luncheons or the lighter side for a formal menu. A number of aspics can be created from fresh vegetable and fruit juices. Most coleslaw recipes can be adapted to include carrot pulp while fruit salads, bean salads, and chicken salads all come alive with a light drizzle of fresh purée over the top.

Be particular about your salad ingredients. Choose simple combinations and couple them to work together, allowing each food to express its individuality.

CUCUMBER, RED BELL PEPPER AND COCONUT SALAD

4 teaspoons sugar
½ cup fresh lime juice
1 to 2 minced jalapeño
   peppers
Salt and white pepper to taste
2 cucumbers, seeded and cut
   into crescents (page 66)
⅓ cup flaked coconut
1 red bell pepper, cut into
   julienne strips

I was introduced to this salad at the home of one of my students, whose family is from the Caribbean. It has a light, refreshingly tart taste and is fat-free. Serve it with spicy dishes for a sweet-hot compliment.

Serves 6

Combine sugar, lime juice, minced jalapeño, salt and white pepper.

Combine cucumber, coconut and red bell pepper in a salad bowl. Pour dressing over salad and toss. Serve chilled.

BLACK BEAN AND RICE SALAD

4 cups water
1½ cups dried black beans,
    washed and picked over
5 whole cloves
1 cinnamon stick
1 teaspoon salt
1½ tablespoons cumin seeds
5 cups cooked rice (about
    2 cups uncooked)
1 cup minced green onions
1 cup minced cilantro
2 tablespoons grated orange
    peel
½ cup orange juice
¼ cup rice vinegar
¼ cup olive oil
2 jalapeño peppers, finely
    minced
Salt and pepper to taste
1 cup mandarin orange slices
½ cup chopped toasted
    pecans

Black beans and rice are a nutritious combination found in several basic cuisines of the world. I like to serve this salad as part of a buffet along with several other salads. It is particularly tasty with barbecued food. Chill ahead of time to let the flavors mingle.

Serves 12 as a side dish

Combine water, beans, cloves, cinnamon stick and salt in large saucepan. Cover and simmer until beans are tender, about 1½ hours. Drain and discard spices.

Place cumin seeds in heavy skillet and stir over medium heat until aromatic, about 2 minutes. Crush seeds in a spice grinder or with mortar and pestle.

Combine beans and rice. Add ground cumin, onion, cilantro, orange peel, orange juice, vinegar, oil and jalapeño. Season with salt and pepper to taste.

Just before serving, stir in oranges and pecans.

MERIDA SALAD

1 large orange
2 tangerines
2 pink grapefruits
1 large green-skinned apple
½ pineapple
2 tablespoons lime juice
⅓ cup fresh cilantro
Salt (optional)

There are several versions of this salad served throughout the Yucatan Peninsula. It's a colorful array of fruits complimented by lime juice and "hot parsley," or cilantro.

Serves 4

Remove peel and white membrane from orange, tangerines and grapefruit. Section fruit. Core and thinly slice apple. Pare and core pineapple; slice into ⅜-inch slices.

On an attractive platter with sloped sides, arrange the sectioned and sliced fruit. Sprinkle lime juice over the fruits and garnish with cilantro. Sprinkle lightly with salt if desired.

TENDER BABY LETTUCES AND WATERCRESS SPRIGS WITH ORANGE CHERVIL BALSAMIC VINAIGRETTE

½ pound baby lettuces
1 bunch watercress, stems removed
⅓ cup walnut oil
⅓ cup salad oil
3 tablespoons balsamic vinegar
¼ cup orange juice
1 teaspoon grated orange peel
1½ tablespoons minced chervil
Salt and pepper to taste
1 cup pink grapefruit sections
½ cup grated daikon radish
½ cup mango purée (2 mangoes)

Watercress adds a spicy freshness to the delicate baby lettuce in this recipe. Look for limestone, Bibb, or curly red leaf lettuces. The rich taste of walnut oil is perfectly balanced by tangy fresh grapefruit, and the crowning touch is a mango purée.

Serves 4

Combine lettuces and watercress leaves.

To make dressing, combine oils, vinegar, orange juice, orange peel, chervil and salt and pepper. Toss salad greens with dressing. Divide among salad plates.

Arrange grapefruit sections attractively on top of salad greens. Sprinkle top with grated radish. Drizzle mango purée lightly over the grapefruit.

TOMATO ASPIC

5 tablespoons gelatin
½ cup cold water
1 cup water
**4 cups tomato juice (about 12
   to 14 tomatoes)**
¾ cup sugar
1½ teaspoons salt
**1 cup Champagne or white
   wine vinegar**
2 teaspoons Worcestershire
**¼ teaspoon liquid hot-pepper
   sauce**
**¼ cup very finely minced
   onion**
2 cups shredded cabbage
2 cups finely chopped celery

Tomato aspic would usually appear at Thanksgiving or Christmas dinner when I was growing up. Although my sisters would always avoid it, I found that aspic complemented all the rich foods served at holiday meals. The slightly tart flavors contrast nicely with the sweetness of the tomatoes. This aspic is beautiful when made in a ring mold, with whole cooked shrimp in the center.

Serves 12 to 16

Combine gelatin and cold water in large mixing bowl. Let stand for 5 minutes.

In medium saucepan, bring water and tomato juice to a boil. Add to softened gelatin and stir to dissolve. Stir in sugar, salt, vinegar, Worcestershire and hot-pepper sauce.

Add onion, cabbage and celery and mix well. Pour into 3-quart mold and chill until set.

GOLDEN HARVEST SALAD

1 pineapple, peeled, cored,
  cut into chunks
4 ripe persimmons, peeled,
  cut into chunks
2 oranges, peeled, membrane
  removed, sectioned
2 papayas, peeled, seeds
  removed, cut into chunks
3 tablespoons lime juice
1 tablespoon honey
2 tablespoons minced mint
Salad greens
½ cup pomegranate seeds
  (optional)

Persimmons are available only from October to January, and the very best are the Japanese variety. The last fruit to stay on the trees in late autumn, persimmons hang on for final ripening after all the leaves have fallen. They are musky, rich and smooth when peeled and eaten fully ripe. This salad is a cornucopia of fall fruits. Serve it on a platter surrounded with colorful fall leaves or on individual plates sprinkled with bright, juicy pomegranate seeds.

Serves 4

Combine fruit in large bowl.

Combine lime juice, wine, honey and mint. Pour over fruit and stir gently. Chill.

Arrange greens on salad plates and spoon fruit mixture on top. Garnish with pomegranate seeds if desired.

SAUERKRAUT, APPLE AND BEET SALAD

2 egg yolks
2 tablespoons apple juice
1 tablespoon lemon juice
1 tablespoon German-style
  mustard
¾ cup olive oil
½ cup vegetable oil
Salt and freshly ground black
  pepper
2 cups sauerkraut, rinsed and
  drained
1 cup julienned beets (about
  3 beets)
1 large Granny Smith apple,
  peeled and grated
½ cup finely chopped red
  onion
2 teaspoons caraway seeds

Don't be afraid to try this version of a cabbage salad. When rinsed, the sauerkraut adds a crunchy, tart element to a winter salad. I like this salad with roast pork, or a charcuterie board filled with sausages and pâtés, dark bread and strong mustards.

Serves 6

Process the egg yolks, apple, lemon juice and mustard in a food processor or blender for 30 seconds. Slowly add the oil while machine is still running, to make a thick mayonnaise. Season to taste with salt and pepper.

Combine the sauerkraut, beets, apple, red onion and caraway seeds in a large bowl. Toss with enough mayonnaise to bind ingredients. Refrigerate and serve chilled.

CITRUS AND GREENS SALAD WITH PINEAPPLE POPPY SEED DRESSING

2 cups red-leaf lettuce leaves
1 cup curly endive pieces
1 bunch watercress sprigs
1 cup orange sections
1 cup grapefruit sections
1 red onion, peeled, sliced
   and separated into rings
1 egg
2 tablespoons lemon juice
¼ cup pineapple juice (about
   ⅓ pineapple)
¼ cup honey
1 tablespoon poppy seeds
1 teaspoon dry mustard
1 teaspoon paprika
1 tablespoon onion juice
   (about ¼ onion)
½ teaspoon salt
¾ cup salad oil

Early in my career, I helped manage the tearoom of a popular department store. Each day, well-dressed shoppers would stop in for a light repast to fuel them through the remainder of their shopping day. Salads were customary, but most in demand was a salad plate with chicken salad and fresh fruit with poppy seed dressing. This recipe calls for a spicy combination of greens tossed with tangy citrus sections. Pass some extra poppy seed dressing for those who want more.

Serves 6

Combine lettuce leaves, endive pieces and watercress sprigs. Add orange, grapefruit and onion and toss.

Place egg, lemon and pineapple juice, honey, poppy seeds, dry mustard, paprika, onion juice and salt in food processor and process until smooth.

Slowly add oil and continue processing. Add quantity of dressing desired to salad and toss.

PAT'S PEPPERED COLESLAW

**3 cups shredded red cabbage
(1 average head)**
1 red bell pepper, diced
**1 cup grated carrot or ½ cup
carrot pulp**
**½ cup finely sliced green
onion**
½ cup mayonnaise
½ cup sour cream
**2 teaspoons grated orange
peel**
**½ cup orange, pineapple or
apricot juice**
**2 teaspoons minced jalapeño
pepper**
Salt and pepper to taste

I particularly like the vibrant colors and surprising flavors in this coleslaw. You can vary the fruit juice you use in the dressing. Try experimenting with pineapple, orange or apricot. Coleslaw improves with three or four hours of chilling.

Serves 6

Combine cabbage, red bell pepper, carrot and green onion.

With food processor or mixer, combine mayonnaise, sour cream, orange peel, juice, jalapeño pepper and salt and pepper to taste.

Chill and serve.

STRAWBERRY HONEYDEW SALAD
WITH RASPBERRY HONEY-LIME DRESSING

¼ cup raspberry nectar
   (¼ pint berries)
2 tablespoons lime juice
1 tablespoon honey
1 pint strawberries, hulled
   and halved lengthwise
1 honeydew melon, cut into
   melon balls
Red leaf lettuce to line salad
   bowl
¼ teaspoon sesame oil
   (optional)

Strawberry growers in Watsonville, California, where I live, claim that it's the strawberry growing capital of the world. The fact is, fresh berries are available here at reasonable prices all summer long, and we use them in as many ways as we can. Brilliant red strawberries team up with a cool, lime-green honeydew for this luscious summer refresher. Tossed in a tart dressing of raspberry, lime and the nutty hint of sesame oil, it becomes a healthful, succulent salad.

Serves 4

Combine the raspberry nectar, lime juice and honey.

Combine strawberries and melon balls and toss lightly with the dressing.

Line an attractive serving bowl with red leaf lettuce and fill with the salad. Sprinkle with sesame oil if desired.

CAESAR-STYLE DRESSING

1 to 2 cloves garlic, minced
6 anchovy fillets
1 cup extra virgin olive oil
¼ cup lemon juice
1 teaspoon creole or Dijon
    mustard
1 tablespoon white wine
    vinegar or sherry vinegar
¼ cup Asiago cheese, grated

Caesar salad has always been a favorite of mine, and my husband makes an excellent one. This dressing has the flavor of caesar dressing but contains no egg. Asiago cheese makes an interesting substitute for Parmesan. If the dressing seems a bit garlicky, you can use less than is called for here. The creole mustard adds a dash of heat.

Makes 1½ cups

In bowl of food processor fitted with metal cutting blade combine garlic, anchovy fillets and ¼ cup olive oil. Process until smooth. Add remaining olive oil, lemon juice, mustard, vinegar and Worcestershire sauce. Add cheese and pulse to combine.

Store in shaker jar in refrigerator.

PINEAPPLE MINT SALAD DRESSING

½ cup pineapple juice
Juice from 2 slices fresh
    ginger (process along with
    pineapple)
1 shallot, peeled (process
    along with pineapple)
½ cup white wine vinegar
2 to 4 tablespoons salad oil
8 to 10 mint leaves, cut
    crosswise into very thin
    strips
¼ teaspoon sesame oil
    (optional)

This salad dressing can be used as a light dressing on greens or to marinate fresh fruits. The addition of sesame oil adds an Asian flavor, but for low-calorie diets, use the smaller amount of oil. Several years ago I purchased pineapple vinegar but have been unable to find it recently. If you should come across it in your travels, purchase a bottle or two to use in salad dressings. You could substitute basil for the mint for an interesting change in flavor.

Makes 1 cup dressing

Combine ingredients in small jar with lid. Shake well before using.

ROASTED PEPPER YOGURT DRESSING

Zest of 1 orange
¼ cup orange juice
¼ cup carrot juice
2 to 3 cloves roasted garlic
 (page 30)
2 tablespoons roasted red
 bell pepper pulp or 1 can
 roasted red bell pepper
1 to 2 teaspoons sugar
⅛ teaspoon salt
½ to 1 teaspoon ground
 cumin
1 cup yogurt

Cucumber slices drizzled with this dressing offer a cool, refreshing summer salad or accompaniment to barbecued food. I also like to compose a salad with sliced cucumber, red onion rings, orange slices and shredded carrot, arranged attractively on salad plates and topped with this dressing. The amount of sugar and cumin to add depends on your personal tastes.

Makes 1¾ cups

Combine all ingredients using food processor or immersion blender.

SAUCES, DIPS AND MARINADES

Owning a catering company has made me a master of crudités. We prepare crisp, crunchy vegetables for parties from ten to one thousand, and it takes an imaginative and quick hand to prepare dip for those numbers. The juice extractor plays a new part in preparing instant flavorings for sauces, dips, and marinades. Rather than finely chopping mountains of garlic, ginger, or onion, use extracts fresh from your juicer to mix with other ingredients.

Peruse your own favorite recipes for sauces and marinades, substituting the juices of cucumbers, peppers, parsley, garlic and ginger as seasonings. Fresh citrus juice makes a tangy marinade for meats, fish and poultry. Imaginative recipes from Mexico and the Caribbean call for luscious combinations of lime, mango, pineapple, and peppers. Your juicer can add limitless dimensions to your backyard barbecues and kitchen grill meals.

Once again, let fun, creativity and your juicer guide you.

SAUCE VERTE

¼ cup cucumber juice (about
⅓ English cucumber)
4 green onions
2 cloves roasted garlic
(page 30)
8 sprigs watercress
½ cup sour cream
½ cup mayonnaise
2 tablespoons minced fresh
dill
½ teaspoon horseradish
Fresh dill, for garnish

For sheer versatility, add this sauce to your repertoire. I have served Sauce Verte with poached or grilled fish, with thickly cut fresh tomatoes, and beautiful eggplant and peppers hot from the grill. For a lovely presentation with crudités, hollow out a red cabbage and fill it with Sauce Verte for dipping. Roasting the garlic gives a softer, more savory flavor than using raw garlic. Be sure to use fresh dill.

Makes 1¼ cups

Extract juice from cucumber, green onions, garlic and watercress. Combine juices.

Combine sour cream and mayonnaise. Add juices, 2 tablespoons dill and horseradish. Mix well. Garnish with fresh dill.

SZECHWAN APRICOT SAUCE

1 cup extracted apricot juice
2 tablespoons honey
1 tablespoon cornstarch
¼ teaspoon ground cin-
namon
⅓ cup hoisin sauce*
¼ teaspoon Szechwan chili
sauce*

*available in Asian markets

This is a sweet, spicy sauce that combines the mellow fresh flavor of apricots with the delicate but mildly hot taste of Szechwan chiles. It's wonderful with grilled fish or stir-fried pork or beef. Serve it with rice and steamed vegetables for an authentic Chinese feast.

Makes 1⅓ cups

Combine apricot juice, honey and cornstarch in a heavy-bottomed saucepan and whisk until smooth. Cook over medium heat, stirring constantly until mixture thickens. Add sauces and stir.

SPICY PEANUT SAUCE

⅓ cup vegetable oil
⅓ cup creamy peanut butter
¼ cup soy sauce
2 tablespoons lemon juice
1 teaspoon sesame oil
Dash of cayenne pepper
2 tablespoons minced green
onions
2 tablespoons minced fresh
cilantro

Once more we have Asian cuisine crossing over to our tables. Peanut sauces are served with Thai noodle dishes, very spicy crab and chiles on spinach salads. My family's been known to dip anything from carrot sticks to pretzels in our peanut sauce. It's that good. Make this sauce ahead of time to allow the flavors to blend.

Makes 1 cup

With food processor or immersion blender, combine all ingredients.

MALTAISE

3 egg yolks
2 tablespoons orange, tangerine or pineapple juice
2 teaspoons grated orange or tangerine peel
¼ teaspoon salt
Pinch of white pepper
¼ pound butter, melted

Maltaise sauce is one of the variations on hollandaise sauce. It usually calls for the addition of orange juice, but here you add tangerine or pineapple juice instead. The rich, fluffy maltaise goes well with poached or lightly grilled fish, egg dishes and steamed vegetables. Using a blender to make the sauce is easy and foolproof. In making a pineapple maltaise, I might substitute 1 teaspoon grated lemon peel for the orange peel.

Makes 1 cup

Place egg yolks, juice, peel, salt and pepper in blender. Blend at high speed for 1 minute.

Remove the center cap of the blender lid and, with blender running, slowly pour in hot melted butter.

Keep sauce warm in a small thermos bottle.

FRESH TOMATO MINT CHUTNEY

⅓ cup minced fresh mint
¼ cup chopped cilantro
1 teaspoon finely grated orange peel
3 tablespoons minced red onion
½ teaspoon salt
1 tablespoon tomato paste
⅓ cup fresh orange or nectarine juice
2 tablespoons fresh lime juice
2 large tomatoes, cut in ½-inch dice
1 tablespoon minced jalapeño pepper

This chutney will remind you of salsa. The two are closely related. For variation, use nectarine juice and one chopped fresh nectarine. It nicely accompanies grilled swordfish or halibut.

Makes about 1½ cups

In medium bowl, combine mint, cilantro, orange peel, red onion and salt. Stir to combine. Add tomato paste, orange or nectarine juice and lime juice. Mix well. Stir in tomatoes and jalapeño. Serve chilled.

AIOLI

3 large cloves garlic, peeled
2 egg yolks
½ teaspoon fine quality
   prepared mustard
¼ teaspoon salt
⅛ teaspoon white pepper
1¼ cups extra virgin olive oil
3 tablespoons lemon juice

Aioli is a gift from the Mediterranean cuisines. It is a garlic-lover's security blanket, to put with almost anything edible. We've used it in soups, as a sauce for fish, as a dip for antipasto assortments, as a sandwich spread. When fresh basil is available, add a tablespoon of finely minced basil leaves.

Makes 1½ cups

Mince garlic in mini chopper or with sharp knife.

Combine garlic, egg yolks, mustard, salt and white pepper in blender or food processor. Slowly add olive oil while blender or processor is still running. After mixture thickens, slowly blend in lemon juice.

RED BELL PEPPER AIOLI

1 recipe aioli
¼ cup red bell pepper pulp
   (pulp from 4 peppers)

If you make the Cream of Roasted Red Bell Pepper Soup (page 59), use this recipe for the pulp.

Combine aioli and red bell pepper pulp.

TARTAR SAUCE

½ jalapeño pepper
½ leek
2 tablespoons cucumber juice
    (about ½ cucumber)
2 tablespoons lemon juice
1½ cups mayonnaise
¾ cup chopped cucumber
2 tablespoons capers, rinsed
    and chopped
½ teaspoon horseradish

Commercially prepared tartar sauce has never appealed to me. If I'm going to take on the calories of tartar sauce, I want it to be freshly prepared and delicious. Vegetable juices give this tartar sauce a fresh, lively flavor.

Makes 2 cups

Process pepper and leek while extracting juice from cucumber. Combine juice with remaining ingredients. Chill.

SUGAR SNAP PEAS WITH MINTED ORANGE DIP

Sugar snap peas
1 cup (8 oz) sour cream
Zest of 1 orange
2 tablespoons orange juice
1 teaspoon ginger juice
1 tablespoon minced mint
1 jalapeño pepper, seeded
    and minced

The joyful thing about sugar snaps is that you eat the whole thing. No pods to throw away, no disappointment when only one pea shows up in a big empty shell. They are sweet as candy, with a crunchy, deep green pea pod announcing the first spring vegetables. Peas lose a bit of their nutrients when cooked, so be sure to blanch them quickly in boiling water and drain and cool immediately. Throwing some ice cubes on them will stop the cooking process.

Combinations of orange, ginger and jalapeño make a lively dip for the peas, giving each crunch a chilly tingle. If you like a smokey flavor, roast the jalapeño briefly before juicing it. When sugar snaps are not available, try this dip with any assortment of crudités.

Makes 1 cup of dip

Blanch snap peas in simmering water for 1 minute; drain and cool. Combine sour cream, orange zest, orange juice, ginger juice, mint and jalapeño.

Place dip in attractive bowl surrounded by sugar snap peas.

CHIPOLTE PEPPER DIP

Zest of 1 orange
3 tablespoons orange juice
½ chipolte pepper, seeded
and minced
1 cup sour cream or yogurt

What better way to treat your guests and family to guiltless, healthful food than an appetizing, colorful array of fresh vegetables served with a beguiling dip? The smokey chipolte chiles combine with orange and yogurt or sour cream as a perfect accompaniment to any crisp fresh vegetable. We've used this dip with grilled shrimp or cold shrimp and found it disappears swiftly. The ingredients are easy to have on hand for an impromptu gathering.

Makes 1¼ cups

Combine all ingredients. Serve chilled.

YOGURT DIP

8 ounces plain yogurt
2 tablespoons fruit nectar or
purée (strawberry, rasp-
berry, peach, apricot,
nectarine, etc.)
1 tablespoon honey
1 teaspoon poppy seeds or
2 teaspoons minced mint

Plain yogurt is like a blank canvas to which you can add the colors and spices you choose. These dips can accompany arrangements of fresh fruit, be drizzled over chopped fresh vegetables or be served with skewers of grilled shrimp or chicken. Use any of the nectars and purées with spices, seeds and herbs to complement them.

Makes 1¼ cups

Combine yogurt, fruit purée, honey and seeds or mint.

ROASTED RED BELL PEPPER DIP

⅓ cup roasted red bell pepper
   pulp
½ cup sour cream
½ cup mayonnaise
2 tablespoons lemon juice
Few drops liquid hot-pepper
   sauce
1 head red cabbage (optional)

The pulp left from processing the juice of roasted red bell peppers can be used to flavor pasta or dip. Here is a colorful dip to present with grilled or cooked prawns or with a basket of crudités.

Makes 1½ cups

Combine red bell pepper pulp, sour cream, mayonnaise, lemon juice and pepper sauce.

For added interest, hollow out red cabbage and fill with the dip.

ROASTED FRESH CHILES OR BELL PEPPERS

Fresh chiles or bell peppers

Cut fresh peppers into quarters. Place on a broiler pan, skin side up, and broil until skin blisters and chars. Remove peppers from pan and place in a paper or plastic bag. Close bag and let peppers sit 15 to 20 minutes. Peel skin off.

Marinades

Fresh fruit juice incorporated into marinades adds a special flavor. Pineapple, citrus and pomegranate are among my favorites. The acid of the fruit juice helps to tenderize less tender cuts of meat. However, tender cuts of meat and poultry need only a short marinating time. Otherwise, the texture becomes too soft.

POMEGRANATE ZINFANDEL MARINADE

1 cup zinfandel wine
1 cup pomegranate juice
2 cloves minced garlic
2 tablespoons hoisin sauce
1 tablespoon rosemary leaves
2 teaspoons minced mint

This is a favorite marinade for rack of lamb or lamb chops. You can also use it for beef and duck.

Combine ingredients in large glass or stainless steel bowl. Marinate tender cuts of meat for 30 minutes. Grill or barbecue according to grill manufacturer's directions.

CITRUS OREGANO MARINADE

1 cup grapefruit juice
1 cup orange juice
¼ cup brown sugar
1 canned chipolte pepper,
    seeds removed
2 teaspoons crushed dried
    oregano
Salt to taste

The chipolte pepper adds a dash of smoke and pepper to this southwestern marinade. A favorite for marinating pork loin roast, you can also use it for chicken and game hens.

Combine ingredients and marinate pork roast for several hours. Discard marinade. Bake at 350° F until internal temperature registers 167° F. For poultry, marinate up to 1 hour before grilling. Combine ½ cup marinade with 2 tablespoons olive oil. Brush poultry pieces as you grill or barbecue.

ENTRÉES

Maybe it doesn't seem likely that your juice extractor can take you beyond juice as far as entrées and other good main dishes. My objective here is to enhance the flavor of some standard dishes with pure fruit and vegetable extracts, and to incorporate the pulps for improved texture and added nutrition.

Carrot and apple pulps are two of the most useable. For some recipes I suggest peeling, seeding, or coring the food before juicing, to make the pulp more uniform. When used in meat marinades, the acids in fruit juice acts as a tenderizer. Meats should not be left for more than 30 minutes in the marinades or the fibers will break down.

Many of these recipes are contemporary versions of favorites from my cooking classes given over the past 12 years. Take some of your own entrées and experiment with fresh juices and pulps to give them a new lift.

VEGETABLE MEDLEY QUICHE

1 9-inch pie shell (recipe
  follows)
1 egg white
½ cup minced shallots,
  about 3
2 tablespoons butter or
  margarine
½ cup diced green bell
  pepper
2 cups sliced mushrooms
1 cup grated Gruyère or Swiss
  cheese
2 eggs
2 egg yolks
1¾ cup half and half
½ cup carrot pulp (3 medium
  carrots)
1 tablespoon chopped fresh
  basil or 1 teaspoon
  crushed fines herbes
½ teaspoon salt
¼ teaspoon white pepper

A quiche is basically a custard filling with an assortment of savory ingredients and cheese, baked until set. You can substitute other vegetables for the mushroom and bell pepper. Broccoli and cauliflower can be used but should be par-boiled until tender. I like to include some bell pepper— red, yellow, green or a combination.

Makes one 9-inch quiche

Preheat oven to 400° F.

Bake pie shell for 5 minutes. Remove from oven and brush with beaten egg white.

Sauté shallots in butter until limp, about 3 minutes. Add green pepper and sauté for 3 minutes. Add mushrooms and sauté until cooked, about 5 minutes. Distribute cooked vegetable mixture in pie shell and sprinkle with ½ cup of the cheese.

Combine eggs, egg yolks and half and half. Stir in carrot pulp, herbs, salt and pepper. Pour over vegetable mixture and sprinkle with remaining cheese.

Bake at 400° F for 10 minutes. Reduce heat to 350° F and bake for 20 to 25 minutes until done.

SINGLE CRUST PASTRY

1⅓ cups sifted all-purpose
  flour
½ teaspoon salt
½ cup vegetable shortening
4 to 5 tablespoons chilled
  water

Makes one 9-inch pie shell

In a medium bowl combine flour and salt. With a pastry blender cut in half of the shortening until mixture is crumbly. Cut in remaining half of shortening (leave some of the pieces of shortening the size of lima beans). Add the water, 1 tablespoon at a time, stirring very lightly with a fork. After 4 tablespoons of water have been added, gather dough into a ball and press. If dough will not form a ball and seems dry, add the remaining 1 tablespoon of water. Gather dough into a ball, press into a flat circle with smooth edges, wrap in plastic and chill for 30 minutes.

On a lightly floured surface roll dough to a circle about 1½ inches larger than pie dish. Carefully pick dough up and gently ease into pie dish (do not stretch the dough). With kitchen scissors trim dough to ¾ inch beyond edge of pie dish; fold under to make a double thickness around the rim and flute with fingers, fork or pastry jagger.

For a single crust baked without filling prick bottom and sides thoroughly with a fork. Bake in a 425° F oven for 10 to 12 minutes, or until golden brown.

For a single crust baked with filling, do not prick dough. Bake according to time and temperature recommended for filling used.

RED BELL PEPPER PASTA WITH SCALLOPS AND ASPARAGUS

2 cloves minced garlic
2 tablespoons butter or
  margarine
1 cup orange juice
1 cup tomato juice (about
  4 Roma tomatoes)
6 to 8 saffron threads dissolved in 2 tablespoons
  warm water
2 teaspoons Tiger Sauce
1 teaspoon fish sauce (nuoc
  mam or nam pla)
1 pound scallops
1 cup cooked asparagus
  pieces
1 pound red bell pasta,
  cooked al dente

A colorful presentation of scallops, the red bell pepper pasta and green asparagus combine to furnish lots of eye appeal, and the flavor of the fresh sauce is delicious. The Tiger Sauce and fish sauce add further interest.

Serves 4

In large frying pan, sauté garlic in butter for 1 to 2 minutes.

Add orange and tomato juice and heat; reduce until mixture becomes thick and somewhat syrupy. Add the dissolved saffron, Tiger Sauce and fish sauce. Add scallops and lightly poach, until just barely cooked.

Add asparagus and heat through. Toss with freshly prepared, cooked red bell pepper pasta.

ROASTED RED BELL PEPPER PASTA

2 tablespoons roasted red
  bell pepper pulp (page 84)
1 teaspoon salt
1 teaspoon Hungarian
  paprika
2 eggs
¾ cup semolina flour
1 cup unbleached all-purpose
  flour

In bowl of food processor, combine red bell pepper pulp, salt, paprika and eggs. Add semolina and all-purpose flour. Process until mixture forms a ball of dough and pulls away from the sides of the work bowl. Process 40 seconds to knead. Turn dough out onto lightly floured surface, cover with plastic wrap and let rest 20 to 30 minutes. When pasta is ready to shape, follow manufacturer's directions for hand-cranked pasta.

SWEDISH MEATBALLS

1 pound ground beef
½ pound ground pork
  sausage
½ cup minced onion
2 tablespoons minced parsley
¼ cup apple pulp
½ cup bread crumbs
1 teaspoon salt
¼ teaspoon ground nutmeg
2 teaspoon Worcestershire
  sauce
1 egg
¼ cup apple juice
¼ cup milk
2 packages meat gravy mix
1 cup apple juice
1 cup half and half

Apple juice and apple pulp add an interesting flavor to this old-time favorite. For a hot appetizer as part of a party buffet, double the recipe. The meat balls may be made ahead of time and frozen. Reheat at 350° F for 6 minutes.

Serves 4

Combine ground beef, sausage, onion, parsley, apple pulp, bread crumbs, salt, nutmeg, Worcestershire, egg, apple juice, and milk. Form into meatballs the size of walnuts.

Place meatballs on jelly roll pans and bake in a 350° F oven until brown and cooked through, about 12 minutes.

In medium saucepan, combine gravy mix with apple juice and half and half and cook until thickened. Stir in meatballs and serve.

ROAST LEG OF LAMB PROVENÇAL

1 5-pound leg of lamb, boned
    and butterflied (ask for
    bones to make broth)
½ cup fruity red wine
¼ cup olive oil
⅓ cup apricot or orange juice
2 teaspoons orange zest
2 tablespoons balsamic
    vinegar
1 teaspoon sugar
2 bay leaves
1 teaspoon crushed thyme
2 teaspoons minced fresh
    rosemary
2 tablespoons capers, rinsed
¼ cup sliced green olives
1 cup pitted prunes
2 cups lamb broth or
    bouillon

This classic from the Mediterranean probably originated on an open fire and hand-turned rotisserie. Roast it on your backyard barbecue and revive some historic culinary legends. Adding wood chips or fruitwood to your fire will impart a savory characteristic to the meat.

Serves 6 to 8

Remove any sinew and excess fat from lamb. Pound thick parts of meat and flatten to an even thickness.

Combine wine, oil, juice, zest, vinegar, sugar, bay leaves, thyme, rosemary, capers, olives and prunes. Place lamb in marinade and marinate for 20 to 30 minutes. (Longer marinating breaks down the muscle fiber, producing a mushy texture.) Prepare barbecue or grill.

Remove lamb from marinade and grill until medium rare. While lamb is grilling, strain marinade and remove bay leaves. Save the strained capers, olives and prunes.

Reduce broth to 1½ cups and add ½ cup drained marinade. Add drained capers, olives and prunes and heat through.

Slice lamb across the grain. Serve with sauce.

LAMB BROTH

Makes 2 cups

Roast lamb bones for 30 minutes at 350° F. Add 2 carrots and ½ onion. Continue roasting for additional 30 minutes. Remove from oven and add 2½ cups water to roasting pan. Scrape up any browned bits and simmer broth for 30 minutes.

BARBEQUED FLANK STEAK

1 cup extracted apple juice
2 tablespoons lemon juice
1 cup soy sauce
½ cup vegetable oil
10 drops liquid smoke
   flavoring
1 bay leaf
2 cloves garlic, finely minced
1 tenderized flank steak (1 to
   1½ lbs)

As the apple season approaches, it can sometimes signal the finale of our summer barbecues. But if you want to stretch one occasion into another, gather the first apples of fall and save enough of the sweet juice to make a marinade. Have a Harvest Moon barbecue one clear October evening to celebrate the enormous bounty the earth gives us each year.

If you have a favorite apple orchard, ask the grower for some dried prunings from the trees. Apple wood imparts a sweet, delicious smokey flavor when used in your barbeque.

Serves 4 to 6

In a shallow dish, combine apple juice, lemon juice, soy sauce, oil, liquid smoke, bay leaf and garlic. Place steak in marinade, cover and refrigerate at least 3 hours. About 1 hour before serving, remove steak from refrigerator, drain marinade and save in covered container. Prepare barbecue. When coals are hot, grill steak until medium rare, about 5 minutes on each side. Slice in thin strips across the grain of the meat.

For a crowd, prepare one recipe marinade for each two flank steaks. Marinade will keep in a covered, refrigerated container for 1 week.

BALSAMIC ROSEMARY CHICKEN

**2 tablespoons pomegranate
juice or orange juice**
**¼ cup pineapple juice (about
⅓ pineapple)**
1 tablespoon honey
**1 tablespoon balsamic
vinegar**
**2 teaspoons minced rose-
mary or rosemary leaves**
**4 chicken breast halves, skin
intact and boned**
Salt and pepper to taste

If you don't yet have a bottle of balsamic vinegar in your pantry, you're in for a treat. Usually imported from Italy, this vinegar is made from red grapes and is aged in wooden casks to impart a unique rich flavor and aroma to anything it touches. I love it in almost all Mediterranean-style dishes, of which this is one. Because the climate in California is so similar to that in Italy, I can grow rosemary quite easily in my northern California garden. It can be seen in great meandering hedges and in kitchen herb pots. Rosemary in flower is a drawing card for bees, and the honey they produce must be a queen's elixir.

This is a quick preparation for chicken that I would either grill or broil after marinating. If you can, use a pomegranate for its slightly tart, refreshing juice. When pomegranates are out of season, use orange juice or any other that you fancy.

Serves 4

Combine pomegranate juice, pineapple juice, honey, vinegar and rosemary. Marinate chicken breasts for 25 to 30 minutes.

Remove chicken from marinade. Salt and pepper lightly. Bake for 15 minutes. While chicken is baking, heat marinade and reduce to a syrupy consistency.

Finish chicken by either broiling or grilling. During last few minutes of cooking, drizzle reduced marinade over chicken.

SMOKEY SOUTHWESTERN CHICKEN

⅓ cup sherry
⅓ cup sliced dried apricots
½ pound chorizo sausage
¼ cup salad oil
6 large boneless chicken
  breasts
1 medium onion, finely
  chopped
1 jalapeño pepper, minced
¾ cup chicken stock, preferably homemade
1 canned chipolte pepper
1 cup tomato juice (3 large)
2 cups peeled, seeded and
  chopped tomatoes
2 cloves garlic, minced
¼ cup lime juice
3 carrots, peeled and cut into
  matchstick pieces
⅓ cup toasted sliced almonds

The smokey complex sauce in this recipe draws its flavor from the chorizo sausage and chipolte pepper, a smoked jalapeño. The sauce in the canned chipoltes can also be used to flavor dips, sauces and entrées. Use a cautious hand; a little goes a very long way.

Serves 6

In small saucepan, heat sherry. Place apricots in small bowl; pour sherry over apricots. Cover and let sit for several hours.

In large skillet or dutch oven, fry chorizo until well cooked and slightly crisp. Remove with slotted spoon and drain on paper towels. Set aside. Discard drippings.

In same skillet heat oil and sauté chicken breasts until well browned on all sides. Remove from pan and set aside.

Add onion and jalapeño pepper to pan and sauté about 3 minutes. Remove from pan and reserve. Drain excess oil. Return pan to heat and add chicken stock. Reduce stock to ½ cup over high heat.

Cut open chipotle pepper and remove seeds. Purée pepper with tomato juice in blender. Add tomato juice and diced tomatoes to skillet along with garlic and cook for several minutes. Add chorizo, chicken breasts, sautéed onion, lime juice and carrots. Cover and simmer for 15 minutes.

Add sherry-soaked apricots and half the almonds; simmer for 5 minutes.

Transfer to serving platter and garnish with remaining almonds.

GROUND TURKEY LOAF

1 pound ground turkey
⅓ cup minced onion
⅓ cup minced celery
⅓ cup carrot pulp
**½ cup quick oatmeal, ground
fine in a food processor or
mini chopper**
¾ teaspoon salt
**2 teaspoons fines herbes,
crushed**
1 egg
½ cup apple juice

Lower in fat than meatloaf made with ground beef, this turkey loaf is delicious served hot or cold. I like to serve it as you would a country pâté, with French bread, Dijon mustard and cornichons (tiny French dill pickles). Take it along on a picnic or serve it as an appetizer.

Makes one 4- by 8-inch loaf

Put ground turkey, onion, celery, carrot pulp, oatmeal, salt and fines herbes in large mixing bowl.

Combine egg and apple juice and add to meat mixture. Mix well and shape into loaf. Place in loaf pan and bake at 350° F for 1 to 1¼ hours.

BRAISED RED CABBAGE

**2 tablespoons butter or
margarine**
¼ cup diced onion
3 cups shredded red cabbage
½ cup apple juice
**2 tablespoons balsamic
vinegar**
2 teaspoons caraway seed

This dish makes a fine accompaniment to beef or poultry.

Serves 4 as an accompaniment

In large sauté pan melt butter. Add onion and sauté for several minutes. Add red cabbage and sauté for 3 to 4 minutes. Add apple juice, vinegar, and caraway. Cover pan with lid and continue to cook until cabbage is done.

POACHED SALMON WITH LEMON-DILL CUCUMBER SAUCE

1 cup water
½ cup dry white wine
1 bay leaf
4 slices lemon
3 large salmon fillets, boned and halved
1 cup sour cream
2 tablespoons fresh lemon juice
2 teaspoons onion juice
2 tablespoons minced fresh dill
1 tablespoon prepared horseradish
½ teaspoon celery salt or celery-based seasoning blend
1 peeled and finely diced English cucumber, placed in colander and drained
Cucumber crescents, for garnish (page 66)

All of us have a version of comfort food that we seek out when times are rough. For some it's pasta, for others a bowl of chicken noodle soup. My mother once prepared a piece of salmon and a baked potato for me when I was feeling a little upset, and salmon has been my comfort food ever since. Fresh salmon is often available in the coastal area where I live and I never tire of it. In the summer I like chilled poached salmon, accompanied by marinated green beans or asparagus tips. This lemon-dill sauce is perfect for poached salmon, served chilled.

Serves 6

Bring to a simmer 1 cup water, the wine, bay leaf and lemon slices. Add salmon fillets; cover and poach until salmon flakes when tested. Keep poaching liquid at a low simmer. Salmon can be chilled in poaching liquid.

In a medium bowl, combine sour cream, lemon and onion juice, dill, horseradish and celery salt. Stir in diced cucumber. Chill for several hours.

To serve, remove salmon from poaching liquid. Serve with cucumber sauce. Garnish with cucumber crescents.

GRILLED SHRIMP WITH SWEET AND SOUR THAI DIPPING SAUCE

Bamboo skewers
1½ pounds medium shrimp,
    peeled and deveined
Oil for basting (2 tablespoons
    peanut or vegetable oil
    mixed with ½ teaspoon
    toasted sesame oil)
¼ cup white wine vinegar
¼ cup pineapple juice (about
    ⅓ pineapple)
2 tablespoons lime juice
⅓ cup sugar
1 jalapeño pepper, minced
¼ cup chopped cucumber
2 tablespoons fish sauce
    (nam pla)
¼ cup chopped roasted
    peanuts

One of my cooking classes was attended by two students from Vietnam. The three of us planned an excursion to Chinatown in downtown Los Angeles to peruse the Asian markets and small specialty shops. We sought out only the freshest and best-quality ingredients to insure the authenticity of our recipes. I was introduced to *nam pla,* the basic fish sauce used in Vietnamese and Thai cooking, which is now available in many fine markets as well as Asian food stores. We ended our outing with an afternoon dim sum and many new food ideas.

Serves 4

Soak bamboo skewers in water for 30 minutes. Prepare barbecue or grill. Remove skewers from water and thread shrimp on the skewers.

Grill shrimp, turning as needed until done.

Combine vinegar, pineapple and lime juice, sugar, jalapeño, cucumber, fish sauce and roasted peanuts. Serve sauce in individual dipping bowls with grilled shrimp.

DESSERTS AND SWEETS

My inspiration for some of the desserts in this chapter comes from the beautiful vessels in which they're served. My daughter and I began collecting glass some time ago (she preferred pink depression glass and I liked green). My passion for small sorbet coupes, delicate parfaits, and dainty cordial glasses encouraged me to create ices, sorbets, parfaits, puddings and purées. My juice extractor is a dessert creator's dream.

The centrifugal extractor yields pure juice. No more straining berries through a sieve — the seeds are extracted as pulp. Even the pulp can be used in the recipes for Fruit And Spice Cookies (page 114) and Chocolate-Chip Apple Cake (page 105). You may have a favorite carrot cake recipe that could use carrot and pineapple pulp from your extractor. If you prefer, make the Pineapple Upside-Down Cake with peaches or apricots. Let your own cravings and the season's best produce inspire you.

Imagine a lovely Champagne coupe with a good vanilla ice cream, layered with fresh fruit purée and accompanied by fruit brandy or liqueur. This could be heaven.

ALOHA APPLE PIE

1½ cups pineapple juice
(2 large)

¾ cup sugar

7 medium cooking apples,
peeled, cored and cut in
¼-inch wedges

3 tablespoons cornstarch

1 tablespoon butter

½ teaspoon vanilla extract

¼ teaspoon salt

1 baked 9-inch pastry shell
(page 91)

½ pint whipping cream

1 to 2 tablespoons sugar

½ cup chopped macadamia
nuts

In the spring and summer, after a fall and winter season of two-crust pies, I like to prepare this light, refreshing version of apple pie.

Makes one 9-inch pie

In a large saucepan bring 1¼ cups pineapple juice and sugar to a boil over medium-high heat. Add apple wedges and cover and simmer until apples are tender but firm, about 6 minutes. Remove apples with slotted spoon.

Combine cornstarch and remaining ¼ cup pineapple juice; add to syrup in saucepan. Cook, stirring, until thickened and bubbly. Remove from heat; add butter, vanilla and salt. Cool 10 minutes.

Pour half of thickened pineapple sauce into baked shell, spreading evenly. Arrange cooked apples in shell; spoon remaining sauce over the top. Chill.

When ready to serve, whip cream until stiff. Flavor with sugar to taste. Garnish pie with whipped cream and chopped nuts.

PINEAPPLE UPSIDE-DOWN CAKE

⅓ cup butter, melted
½ cup brown sugar
½ cup fresh pineapple,
    peeled, cored and sliced
    into ¼-inch slices
12 maraschino cherries
1⅓ cups flour
¾ cup sugar
2 teaspoons baking powder
¼ teaspoon baking soda
½ teaspoon ground mace
½ teaspoon salt
⅓ cup softened butter
⅓ cup pineapple pulp
⅓ cup milk
⅓ cup fresh pineapple juice
    (about ½ pineapple)
1 teaspoon vanilla
1 egg
Whipped cream, for garnish

Even a traditional dessert such as this can be enhanced by using fresh pineapples and juice. When you choose fresh pineapples, look for a glow of golden color and a nice aroma. If you need to further ripen the pineapple, do not refrigerate it, but keep it upside down in a warm place to let the juices run down through the fruit. Mace is a sweet, pungent spice that comes from the net-like covering of a seed we call nutmeg. The English use mace to flavor fruit-cakes, cheeses and potted meats.

Makes one 8-inch square cake

Preheat oven to 325° F. Combine melted butter and brown sugar in 8-inch pan. Arrange slices of pineapple and cherries in attractive design over butter-sugar mixture.

In large mixing bowl, combine flour, sugar, baking powder, baking soda, mace and salt.

Add softened butter, pineapple pulp, milk, pineapple juice and vanilla, and beat for 2 minutes at medium speed on mixer. Scrape sides and bottom of bowl frequently. Add egg and beat 2 more minutes.

Pour batter over fruit. Bake for 40 minutes. Remove from oven and allow to cool for 1 minute. Invert onto serving plate. Allow pan to remain over cake for a few minutes to keep the fruit and syrup in place. Remove pan and serve cake while still warm, passing whipped cream if desired.

BLACKBERRY SUPREME CAKE

1¾ cups flour
1 cup sugar
2½ teaspoons baking powder
½ teaspoon soda
½ teaspoon salt
⅓ cup soft butter
½ cup blackberry juice
½ teaspoon vanilla
½ cup milk
1 large egg
⅓ cup blackberry liqueur
1 cup whipping cream
1 tablespoon sugar
3 ripe nectarines, sliced

If you have someone special with a July or August birthday, making this cake would show you truly care. The cake is simple, but the flavors are scrumptious. Use fresh blackberry juice for a deep purple cake, slightly sweet and moist. With a bite of fresh nectarine and sweetened whip cream, it will melt in your mouth and into your memory. This is a summer cake for any delicious occasion.

Makes a single-layer 9-inch cake

Preheat oven to 350° F. Grease and flour a 9-inch baking pan.

Blend together flour, sugar, baking powder, soda and salt. Add butter and blackberry juice and beat 2 minutes on medium speed. Scrape sides and bottom of bowl frequently. Add milk and egg and beat 2 more minutes, scraping bowl.

Pour batter into well-greased square baking pan. Bake for 30 to 35 minutes.

Cool cake. Turn out of pan and place on cake plate. Prick top of cake and drizzle blackberry liqueur over the top.

Whip cream and sweeten with 1 tablespoon sugar.

Split cake and fill with half of the whipped cream and sliced nectarines. Place top layer on cake and frost with remaining whipped cream.

CHOCOLATE-CHIP APPLE CAKE

3 eggs
¾ cup butter or margarine
1¾ cups sugar
¼ cup apple pulp (about
  2 apples)
¾ cup milk
2 teaspoons vanilla
2½ cups flour
3 tablespoons cocoa
1 teaspoon baking soda
1 teaspoon cinnamon
½ teaspoon allspice
1 cup walnuts
½ cup semi-sweet chocolate
  chips
Sweetened whipped cream

When I use apple pulp in a recipe, I always peel the apples and remove the core before processing the apple for juice. The resulting pulp will be more uniform in texture. This cake is especially moist and flavorful with the addition of apple pulp.

Makes one 9- by 13-inch sheet cake or one small bundt cake

Preheat oven to 325° F for glass baking dish, or 350° F for metal bundt cake pan.

Cream together the eggs, sugar, apple pulp, butter, milk and vanilla.

Sift together the flour, cocoa, baking soda, cinnamon and allspice. Add to creamed mixture and mix well. Fold in walnuts and chocolate chips.

Spoon into greased and floured pan. Bake 30 minutes for sheet cake or 50 to 60 minutes for bundt pan, or until cake tests done.

Serve with a dollop of whipped cream.

FRESH FRUIT AMBROSIA IN PINEAPPLE SHELLS

1 fresh pineapple
1 pint strawberries, washed
and hulled.
2 peaches, peeled and sliced
½ cup toasted almond slivers
1 cup strawberry nectar
(1½ pints berries)
2 tablespoons brown sugar
1 tablespoon orange juice
2 tablespoons Grand Marnier
½ cup toasted coconut, for
garnish

This dessert makes its appearance in its own carved shell. Your guests or family will feel that you've treated them with extra care when they see the colorful presentation. When preparing fresh pineapple for juice, cut the pineapple in half lengthwise, then make one more lengthwise cut to make four quarters, leaving the top green leaves attached. With a sharp knife, remove the flesh of the pineapple, leaving four individual shells.

Serves 4

Prepare pineapple shells. Remove core from pineapple pieces and cut into chunks. Combine the pineapple chunks, strawberries, peaches and almonds. Divide the fruits among the 4 shells.

Combine strawberry nectar, brown sugar, orange juice and Grand Marnier and drizzle over the fruits. Garnish tops with toasted coconut.

RASPBERRY COUSCOUS PARFAIT

½ cup apple juice (2 medium
    apples)
½ cup pineapple juice
    (½ large pineapple)
½ cup couscous
1 cup raspberry purée (1 pint
    berries)
2 tablespoons Kirsch
2 tablespoons sugar
1 cup crème anglaise (see
    below)
1½ pints whole raspberries

Couscous is a Moroccan grain with a fine texture. When served as a breakfast cereal, it resembles cream of wheat but is more interesting. Couscous adds a lovely softness to this parfait. When layered with raspberry purée, fresh berries, and crème anglaise, it's a knockout for the eyes and the appetite.

Serves 4

Combine apple and pineapple juice in saucepan and heat just to boil. Add couscous, stir, cover and set off heat. When couscous has cooled, chill mixture well.

Combine raspberry purée, Kirsch and sugar. Prepare parfaits by alternating layers of the prepared couscous, raspberry purée, crème anglaise and the whole berries in parfait glasses or stemmed goblets.

CREME ANGLAISE

3 egg yolks
⅓ cup granulated sugar
1¼ cups hot milk
2 teaspoons vanilla extract
1 to 2 tablespoons rum
1 tablespoon softened butter

In heavy-bottomed saucepan, whisk egg yolks until lemon-colored. Gradually stir in the sugar, then stir in the milk.

Cook over low heat, stirring constantly, until sauce thickens enough to coat a metal spoon. Do not let the sauce simmer or it will curdle.

Remove from heat and stir in vanilla, rum and butter.

MANGO MELBA SUNDAE

4 ripe peach halves, peeled
1 cup mango purée (about
   3 mangoes)
1 cup raspberry purée (1 pint
   raspberries)
1 pint fine-quality vanilla ice
   cream
Whole raspberries, for
   garnish

Despite their alluring tropical flavor, mangos can be a challenge. They come in all sorts of shapes, weights, and hues and from many parts of the world. Mangoes are grown in India, Central America, the Caribbean, and Florida, but they are all equally difficult to get into. Because the mango has a tenacious hold on its seed, a ripe fruit can be utterly destroyed in the process of freeing it from the seed. Try cutting straight down alongside the seed to produce two meaty halves. Then trim the small remaining wedges away from the seed as cleanly as possible. When extracting juice from the mango, you will have a luscious golden purée. Mangoes are frequently served with a tart wedge of lime, but in this case the raspberry purée provides that pleasantly piquant touch. The original Melba included a lightly poached peach half, but we like this dessert with a juicy fresh summer peach.

Serves 4

Arrange peach halves in attractive dessert bowls. Place a scoop of vanilla ice cream in each half. Drizzle with the mango and raspberry purées. Garnish top with fresh whole raspberries.

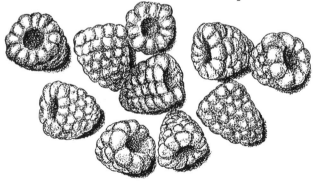

STRAWBERRIES YIN YANG

2 pints strawberries
½ pint (8 oz) sour cream or
plain yogurt
1 tablespoon extracted ginger
juice
2 tablespoons lime juice
1 tablespoon brown sugar
Zest of 1 orange
2 teaspoons mint, chopped
fine

Since fresh strawberries are available to us twelve months each year, this dessert can be served at a Memorial Day barbecue or a Christmas brunch. Strawberries in winter come to us from elsewhere in the world, but they are no less appreciated at that time than when personally hand-picked in June. Fresh ginger and lime in combination is an exotic complement to the sweet whole berries. Yogurt gives a slightly more tart accent to the sauce than sour cream. This is a low-calorie, easy to digest, nutrient-packed surprise in an elegant dessert. Serve it often and make the portions generous.

Serves two

Remove hulls from strawberries. Divide between 2 attractive fruit bowls or stemmed goblets.

Combine sour cream, ginger juice, lime juice, brown sugar, orange zest and mint, whisk until smooth.

Spoon sauce over strawberries. Garnish with fresh mint leaves.

FRESH FRUIT TRIFLE

1 prepared pound cake
½ cup sherry or liqueur of
   your choice
5 peaches, peeled and sliced
   or 4 bananas, sliced
1 recipe crème anglaise
   (page 107)
1 recipe raspberry coulis
   (see below)
1 cup whipping cream
2 tablespoons sugar
1½ pints fresh raspberries,
   for garnish

When I think of trifle, I think of glorious holiday buffets brimming with foods made specially for festive crowds and eager palates. There, by the desserts, might be an elegant glass bowl layered with delicate cake, fluffy custard, and juicy, brilliant fruits. This is trifle. Sherry is a customary ingredient used to soak and soften the cake. You can vary the recipe by using fruits, jams, and liqueurs of your choice. And you can make any holiday an occasion to present this extraordinary dessert.

Serves 8

Slice pound cake into ½-inch slices. Brush each slice with sherry or liqueur.

Select an attractive glass or crystal serving bowl. Line the sides and bottom with pound cake slices.

Add a layer of sliced peaches. Spoon ⅓ of the crème anglaise and the raspberry coulis over the sliced peaches. Continue layering pound cake slices, peaches and sauces.

Whip the cream and sweeten with sugar. Spread over the top of the trifle. Garnish with raspberries.

DESSERT SAUCES

Fresh fruit and a juice extractor are the basic ingredients to create a delightful crowning for a simple dessert. You can invent a myriad of toppings and sauces to be served over warm cake, fresh fruits, puddings and ice cream. Here are a few to get you started.

BERRY COULIS

2 cups berry purée
2 to 4 tablespoons sugar
2 tablespoons Grand Marnier
   or Kirsch

Stir to combine and spoon over dessert.

MANGO OR PAPAYA COULIS

2 cups mango or papaya purée
2 tablespoons sugar
1 tablespoon lime juice
2 tablespoons Grand Marnier

Stir to combine and spoon over dessert.

MELBA SAUCE

1 cup raspberry purée
½ cup currant jelly
¼ cup sugar
2 tablespoons cold water
1 tablespoon cornstarch

In medium stainless steel saucepan, bring raspberry purée, currant jelly and sugar to a boil. Combine cold water and cornstarch and whisk into raspberry mixture. Cook 1 minute.

Cool and refrigerate.

LEMON SAUCE

½ cup sugar
1 tablespoon cornstarch
1 cup water
2 tablespoons butter
1½ tablespoons lemon juice
Dash of grated nutmeg

In saucepan, combine sugar and cornstarch. Add water gradually, stirring constantly. Cook until thickened, about 5 minutes. Remove from heat and stir in butter, lemon juice and nutmeg.

ORANGE SAUCE

1 cup sugar
¼ teaspoon salt
2 tablespoons cornstarch
2 teaspoons grated orange rind
¾ cup water
1 cup orange juice
¼ cup lemon juice
2 tablespoons butter
1 to 2 tablespoons Grand Marnier (optional)

In saucepan, combine sugar, salt, cornstarch and orange rind. Add water gradually. Stir in orange juice. Bring to a boil and cook until thickened, stirring constantly. Remove from heat and add lemon juice, butter and Grand Marnier if desired.

FRUIT SORBETS

Fruit ices have a long history. Auguste Escoffier offered recipes for glacés that were similar to our sherbets of today. In Italy, granité was made with a coarser texture and served between courses of a meal. The sorbets we know today are made in a shallow pan, stirred frequently while they are freezing and use tantalizing combinations of fruit, herbs and liqueurs.

In creating sorbets, I like to freeze the mixtures and then process them with a food processor. Add lemon or lime juice for a zesty touch. I've achieved some interesting flavors by steeping 1 to 2 tablespoons of herbs in ¼ cup hot water, then adding the strained liquid to the sorbet before freezing. Rosemary, basil and sage work nicely.

TANGERINE SORBET

2½ cups tangerine juice
½ cup cold sugar syrup
1 tablespoon lemon or lime juice

LEMON SORBET

¾ cup lemon juice
1½ cups water
1 cups cold sugar syrup

STRAWBERRY, RASPBERRY OR BLACKBERRY SORBET

2 cups strawberry, raspberry or blackberry nectar
⅓ cup cold sugar syrup
1 tablespoon lemon juice

MANGO SORBET

2 cups mango purée
½ cup cold sugar syrup
1 tablespoon lime juice
2 tablespoons Grand Marnier

Combine ingredients listed for selected sorbet and mix well. Pour into shallow baking dish and freeze until firm.

Remove from freezer and allow to soften slightly. Cut into chunks and process in food processor until smooth.

BERRY WINE SORBET

2 cups zinfandel or dry premium red wine
½ cup sugar
1 tablespoon lemon zest
1 cinnamon stick
1 cup berry purée (blackberries or raspberries are best)
1 tablespoon lemon juice
1 tablespoon blackberry or raspberry liqueur

Sorbets are a refreshing end to any meal, particularly if the courses have been rich or spicy. Serve a sorbet as a small course after a rich appetizer or entrée to refresh the palate. This recipe makes a lovely presentation if scooped into a poached pear half.

Serves 4

In a stainless steel saucepan, combine wine, sugar, lemon zest and cinnamon stick. Bring to a boil. Reduce heat and simmer 5 minutes. Cool mixture and strain.

Stir in berry purée, lemon juice and liqueur. Pour mixture into shallow baking dish and freeze until solid.

When ready to serve, remove from freezer, soften slightly, and cut into chunks. Process in food processor until smooth.

Serve scoops of sorbet in stemmed goblets, sherbet glasses or hollowed-out orange or lemon shells.

FRUIT AND SPICE COOKIES

1 cup brown sugar
¾ cup butter or margarine
1 egg
1 teaspoon vanilla
⅔ cup pineapple pulp
3 cups flour
2 teaspoons cinnamon
½ teaspoon ground ginger
½ teaspoon ground nutmeg
½ teaspoon ground cloves
½ teaspoon salt
½ teaspoon baking soda
1 cup golden raisins
1 cup chopped pecans

Processing pineapples for juice produces a quantity of pulp. The consistency of the pulp is so much like applesauce that it sent me back into my recipe files to look for a family heirloom. On a fingerprinted 3 by 5 card was my grandmother's recipe for Applesauce Cookies. These cookies are soft and chewy, full of flavor and texture. Using pineapple pulp has given one of our favorite recipes a new taste.

Makes 3 dozen 2½-inch cookies or 4 dozen smaller cookies

Preheat oven to 350° F.

In a large bowl, thoroughly combine sugar, butter, egg and vanilla. Add pineapple pulp and mix well.

Sift together the flour, cinnamon, ginger, nutmeg, cloves, salt and baking soda. Add to butter-sugar mixture and combine well. Stir in the raisins and pecans.

Use a rounded tablespoonful and place 1 inch apart on well-greased cookie sheets. Bake for 12 to 15 minutes.

CARROT RAISIN MUFFINS

1¼ cup Bran Buds
½ cup golden raisins
½ cup carrot pulp
1¼ cups milk
1¼ cups flour
⅓ cup sugar
1 tablespoon baking powder
½ teaspoon salt
½ teaspoon nutmeg
½ teaspoon ground cinnamon
1 egg
¼ cup oil

When I know I'm going to make these muffins, I peel the carrots before extracting the juice. The pulp seems to be more consistent in appearance and texture. This recipe could be varied by substituting nuts or chocolate chips for the raisins.

One dozen muffins

In a large bowl, combine Bran Buds, raisins and carrot pulp. Add milk and stir.

Combine flour, sugar, baking powder, salt, nutmeg and cinnamon.

Whisk egg and oil together. Add flour mixture and egg mixture to pulp mixture, and mix well.

Portion into muffin tins and bake at 400° F for 18 to 20 minutes.

APPENDICES

NUTRITIONAL CHART OF RECIPES

The nutritional values shown below are derived from the complete list of ingredients for each recipe. To find the proper nutritional values for any recipe that calls for more than one serving you need to divide the total figure by the number of servings for that particular recipe. For instance, the recipe for A Special Sangria calls for 4 servings, so you would divide the following nutritional totals by 4 in order to arrive at the proper totals for an individual serving. The following is an example of this procedure:

A Special Sangria (Complete Recipe)   1,529   7.9   2.5   184.3   89
Percentage of Calories derived from Fats: 1.50%
A Special Sangria (Individual Serving)   382   1.9   0.6   46.07   22
Percentage of Calories derived from Fats: 0.37%

In addition, the sodium values shown below do not account for the use of optional salt or salt seasoning called for in a number of recipes.

	CAL. (GMS)	PROT. (GMS)	FAT (GMS)	SUGAR (GMS)	SODM. (MGS)
FRUIT JUICES					
Apricot Blush	136	2.7	1.0	32.5	3
Percentage of Calories derived from Fats: 6.91%					
The Blushing Pear	215	2.3	1.3	44.3	6
Percentage of Calories derived from Fats: 5.44%					
Pear Plum Sweet-Tart	217	2.8	0.7	56.7	5
Percentage of Calories derived from Fats: 2.90%					
Pineapple Grapefruit Juice	124	1.5	0.6	31.6	3
Percentage of Calories derived from Fats: 4.44%					
Ambrosial Delight	144	1.5	1.0	36.5	12
Percentage of Calories derived from Fats: 6.15%					
Minted Blueberry "Dew"	161	3.2	1.6	37.5	39
Percentage of Calories derived from Fats: 8.69%					
Summer Harvest	177	3.2	1.9	42.1	4
Percentage of Calories derived from Fats: 9.58%					
Autumn Harvest	201	2.0	1.5	50.1	11
Percentage of Calories derived from Fats: 6.72%					
Apple Strawberry Delight	178	2.2	2.0	42.5	6
Percentage of Calories derived from Fats: 10.11%					
Cranapple Splash	149	1.3	1.7	36.6	6
Percentage of Calories derived from Fats: 9.97%					
Pink Zinger	267	5.6	1.9	48.8	8
Percentage of Calories derived from Fats: 6.26%					
Over The Rainbow	316	3.6	1.6	53.6	6
Percentage of Calories derived from Fats: 4.68%					
The Setting Sun	135	2.4	2.0	30.8	4
Percentage of Calories derived from Fats: 13.34%					
Melon Medley	292	6.1	2.7	70.1	43
Percentage of Calories derived from Fats: 8.46%					

	CAL. (GMS)	PROT. (GMS)	FAT (GMS)	SUGAR (GMS)	SODM. (MGS)
Fire And Ice	226	4.4	1.6	55.2	10
Percentage of Calories derived from Fats: 6.49%					
Harvest Glow	163	2.0	2.0	37.8	7
Percentage of Calories derived from Fats: 10.85%					
Coconut Tangerine	256	3.7	1.2	63.6	25
Percentage of Calories derived from Fats: 4.05%					
Coconut, Orange, Papaya	194	1.6	1.6	47.8	20
Percentage of Calories derived from Fats: 7.48%					
Coconut Pineapple	64	1.4	0.7	44.3	23
Percentage of Calories derived from Fats: 9.47%					
Coconut Peach	180	2.6	0.8	48.4	18
Percentage of Calories derived from Fats: 3.78%					
Tropical Sun	232	1.9	1.1	57.5	30
Percentage of Calories derived from Fats: 4.08%					
Red, White And Blue	76	1.1	0.7	16.7	17
Percentage of Calories derived from Fats: 8.23%					
VEGETABLE JUICES					
Vita Cocktail	116	5.0	0.9	24.3	51
Percentage of Calories derived from Fats: 6.89%					
T.N.T. Cocktail	218	3.3	0.7	54.2	11
Percentage of Calories derived from Fats: 2.89%					
It's Italian	116	5.5	1.0	24.6	18
Percentage of Calories derived from Fats: 7.39%					
Tiger Tom	85	3.0	0.6	18.9	31
Percentage of Calories derived from Fats: 6.05%					
Summer Salad In A Glass	114	6.5	1.0	23.4	5
Percentage of Calories derived from Fats: 7.80%					

	CAL. (GMS)	PROT. (GMS)	FAT (GMS)	SUGAR (GMS)	SODM. (MGS)
Zippy Green And Green	50	2.5	0.2	12.0	164
Percentage of Calories derived from Fats: 3.98%					
The Green Goddess	48	1.3	0.2	8.7	614
Percentage of Calories derived from Fats: 3.17%					
Smokey Joe	217	5.7	0.8	30.6	36
Percentage of Calories derived from Fats: 3.40%					
La Provence	108	5.0	0.9	22.2	13
Percentage of Calories derived from Fats: 7.51%					
Carrot Ginger Splash	127	3.6	0.6	30.4	71
Percentage of Calories derived from Fats: 3.97%					
Pure Gold	186	3.3	0.8	48.2	20
Percentage of Calories derived from Fats: 3.63%					
The Underground	84	2.2	0.4	18.9	96
Percentage of Calories derived from Fats: 4.03%					
A Hot Tamale	209	8.4	2.2	46.8	14
Percentage of Calories derived from Fats: 9.47%					
Cucumber Buttermilk Flip	130	5.5	4.6	15.0	73
Percentage of Calories derived from Fats: 31.50%					
Borscht Cocktail	81	4.2	1.4	11.9	90
Percentage of Calories derived from Fats: 15.25%					

JUICE DRINKS

	CAL. (GMS)	PROT. (GMS)	FAT (GMS)	SUGAR (GMS)	SODM. (MGS)
Pineapple Agua Fresca	229	1.5	0.8	59.9	3
Percentage of Calories derived from Fats: 2.95%					
Strawberry Peach Agua Fresca	147	2.7	1.7	35.2	5
Percentage of Calories derived from Fats: 10.41%					
Mango Agua Fresca	448	4.2	2.4	114.2	42
Percentage of Calories derived from Fats: 4.82%					
Kumquat Agua Fresca	268	2.3	70.2	18	
Percentage of Calories derived from Fats: 0.00%					
Watermelon Agua Fresca	314	4.2	1.6	78.3	8
Percentage of Calories derived from Fats: 4.58%					
Strawberry Liquado	242	4.0	3.7	51.8	32
Percentage of Calories derived from Fats: 13.84%					
Peach Liquado	235	4.1	2.4	56.6	31
Percentage of Calories derived from Fats: 9.28%					
Pineapple Liquado	314	5.1	4.9	67.8	58
Percentage of Calories derived from Fats: 13.91%					
Pink Flamingo Glace	319	4.0	1.9	54.0	10
Percentage of Calories derived from Fats: 5.37%					
Lemon Strawberry Chamomile Tea	220	2.7	2.2	51.2	13
Percentage of Calories derived from Fats: 9.00%					
Jamaica Flower Tea	4	6		6	
Percentage of Calories derived from Fats: 0.00%					
Strawberry Jamaica Flower Tea	140	1.5	1.2	32.9	10
Percentage of Calories derived from Fats: 7.73%					
Pineapple Jamaica Flower Tea	119	0.6	0.6	30.7	3
Percentage of Calories derived from Fats: 4.62%					
Tangerine Jamaica Flower Tea	123	1.8	0.5	31.3	6
Percentage of Calories derived from Fats: 3.65%					
Lemon Mint Spritzer	754	0.4	0.1	180.5	65
Percentage of Calories derived from Fats: 0.12%					

	CAL. (GMS)	PROT. (GMS)	FAT (GMS)	SUGAR (GMS)	SODM. (MGS)
Kiwi Spritzer	235	0.4	0.2	9.5	41
Percentage of Calories derived from Fats: 0.83%					
Ginger Pineapple Kiwi Spritzer	154	0.5	0.2	13.6	35
Percentage of Calories derived from Fats: 1.17%					
Strawberry Spritzer	206	2.9	2.3	44.7	23
Percentage of Calories derived from Fats: 10.05%					

HERBAL SYRUPS

	CAL. (GMS)	PROT. (GMS)	FAT (GMS)	SUGAR (GMS)	SODM. (MGS)
Orange Basil	341	2.6	0.3	85.5	7
Percentage of Calories derived from Fats: 0.69%					
Pineapple Rosemary	399	0.7	0.9	112.7	5
Percentage of Calories derived from Fats: 0.88%					

SMOOTHIES

	CAL. (GMS)	PROT. (GMS)	FAT (GMS)	SUGAR (GMS)	SODM. (MGS)
Strawberry Banana Smoothie	648	51.5	13.5	47.8	456
Percentage of Calories derived from Fats: 18.79%					
Orange Prune Smoothie	374	22.3	1.3	38.4	308
Percentage of Calories derived from Fats: 3.06%					
Pineapple Smoothie	596	44.4	8.7	51.4	453
Percentage of Calories derived from Fats: 13.10%					
Mango Melba Smoothie	814	36.8	4.5	127.2	487
Percentage of Calories derived from Fats: 5.01%					
Summer Medley Smoothie	546	24.7	1.1	89.3	310
Percentage of Calories derived from Fats: 1.77%					
Purple Cow	335	22.2	1.4	32.7	315
Percentage of Calories derived from Fats: 3.80%					
Peaches 'N' Cream	242	7.5	2.1	48.9	146
Percentage of Calories derived from Fats: 7.63%					
Blueberries 'N' Cream	346	4.6	12.0	61.3	43
Percentage of Calories derived from Fats: 31.25%					

PARTY DRINKS

	CAL. (GMS)	PROT. (GMS)	FAT (GMS)	SUGAR (GMS)	SODM. (MGS)
Very Berry Royale	806	4.4	3.9	50.3	365
Percentage of Calories derived from Fats: 4.35%					
Raspberry Punch	734	7.2	6.6	86.2	19
Percentage of Calories derived from Fats: 8.09%					
Ginger Strawberry Pineapple Punch	1,530	8.0	5.8	38.2	72
Percentage of Calories derived from Fats: 3.44%					
A Special Sangria	1,529	7.9	2.5	184.3	89
Percentage of Calories derived from Fats: 1.50%					

SOUPS

	CAL. (GMS)	PROT. (GMS)	FAT (GMS)	SUGAR (GMS)	SODM. (MGS)
Ginger Carrot Squash Bisque	498	14.6	29.6	41.5	1565
Percentage of Calories derived from Fats: 53.51%					
Cream of Roasted Red Bell Pepper Soup	405	15.7	9.5	68.1	1763
Percentage of Calories derived from Fats: 16.91%					
Cream of Tomato Basil Soup	504	23.2	10.9	86.5	763
Percentage of Calories derived from Fats: 19.52%					
Avocado Gazpacho	1,319	40.8	57.3	183.4	2179
Percentage of Calories derived from Fats: 39.10%					

	CAL. (GMS)	PROT. (GMS)	FAT (GMS)	SUGAR (GMS)	SODM. (MGS)
Watermelon Gazpacho	451	12.3	3.0	105.0	174
Percentage of Calories derived from Fats: 5.89%					
Asian Gazpacho	341	17.4	14.9	31.4	3005
Percentage of Calories derived from Fats: 39.17%					
Pineapple Peach Soup	852	6.4	2.6	173.6	12
Percentage of Calories derived from Fats: 2.75%					
Strawberry Ginger Soup With Berries	544	9.3	6.7	118.6	18
Percentage of Calories derived from Fats: 11.01%					
Melon Soup With Strawberries	2,021	10.0	4.7	181.3	518
Percentage of Calories derived from Fats: 2.09%					
Quick Borscht	209	7.4	3.8	39.4	1940
Percentage of Calories derived from Fats: 16.37%					
Chilled Cucumber Soup With Shrimp And Dill	209	18.5	1.3	34.7	740
Percentage of Calories derived from Fats: 5.77%					
Tomato Clam Chowder	798	53.0	20.0	107.6	1299
Percentage of Calories derived from Fats: 22.57%					

SALADS AND SALAD DRESSINGS

	CAL. (GMS)	PROT. (GMS)	FAT (GMS)	SUGAR (GMS)	SODM. (MGS)
Cucumber, Red Bell Pepper And Coconut Salad	449	5.1	13.6	74.7	728
Percentage of Calories derived from Fats: 27.24%					
Black Bean And Rice Salad	2,783	38.9	154.2	304.6	6661
Percentage of Calories derived from Fats: 49.88%					
Merida Salad	533	6.9	2.0	133.9	20
Percentage of Calories derived from Fats: 3.34%					
Tender Baby Lettuces And Watercress Sprigs With Orange Chervil Balsamic Vinaigrette	1,078	8.4	75.8	93.4	667
Percentage of Calories derived from Fats: 63.29%					
Tomato Aspic	1,392	50.7	4.2	257.5	3554
Percentage of Calories derived from Fats: 2.73%					
Golden Harvest Salad	1,075	15.7	3.7	269.1	54
Percentage of Calories derived from Fats: 3.10%					
Sauerkraut, Apple And Beet Salad	2,890	12.3	299.7	68.9	2972
Percentage of Calories derived from Fats: 93.33%					
Citrus And Greens With Pineapple Poppy Seed Dressing	2,292	23.0	200.7	152.8	1401
Percentage of Calories derived from Fats: 78.79%					
Pat's Peppered Coleslaw	689	14.5	42.6	77.5	1361
Percentage of Calories derived from Fats: 55.65%					
Strawberry Honeydew Salad With Raspberry Honey-Lime Dressing	484	8.2	5.6	114.7	151
Percentage of Calories derived from Fats: 10.32%					
Caesar-Style Dressing	2,375	32.0	244.0	11.5	895
Percentage of Calories derived from Fats: 92.48%					

	CAL. (GMS)	PROT. (GMS)	FAT (GMS)	SUGAR (GMS)	SODM. (MGS)
Pineapple Mint Salad Dressing	572	1.8	42.8	49.9	7
Percentage of Calories derived from Fats: 67.35%					
Roasted Pepper Yogurt Dressing	343	15.3	5.7	56.7	473
Percentage of Calories derived from Fats: 14.98%					

SAUCES, DIPS AND MARINADES

	CAL. (GMS)	PROT. (GMS)	FAT (GMS)	SUGAR (GMS)	SODM. (MGS)
Sauce Verte	543	6.0	51.9	17.4	71
Percentage of Calories derived from Fats: 85.97%					
Szechwan Apricot Sauce	348	9.5	0.8	58.4	7806
Percentage of Calories derived from Fats: 2.02%					
Spicy Peanut Sauce	773	16.2	80.2	10.3	2273
Percentage of Calories derived from Fats: 93.36%					
Maltaise	1,021	78.8	106.5	8.9	636
Percentage of Calories derived from Fats: 93.88%					
Fresh Tomato Mint Chutney	186	5.5	1.4	33.6	1223
Percentage of Calories derived from Fats: 6.68%					
Aioli	2,642	51.9	290.5	5.7	653
Percentage of Calories derived from Fats: 98.96%					
Red Bell Pepper Aioli	2,698	54.7	290.9	17.7	685
Percentage of Calories derived from Fats: 97.04%					
Tartar Sauce	2,055	2.9	240.5	18.2	227
Percentage of Calories derived from Fats: 105.30%					
Minted Orange Dip For Sugar Snap Peas	526	8.0	44.2	14.0	105
Percentage of Calories derived from Fats: 75.57%					
Chipolte Pepper Dip	199	13.7	5.3	21.9	200
Percentage of Calories derived from Fats: 23.89%					
Yogurt Dip	411	18.3	17.7	36.3	205
Percentage of Calories derived from Fats: 38.70%					
Roasted Red Bell Pepper Dip	1,137	2.3	122.9	7.4	32
Percentage of Calories derived from Fats: 97.32%					
Pomegranate Zinfandel Marinade	341	4.9	1.8	1.2	2627
Percentage of Calories derived from Fats: 4.75%					
Citrus Oregano Marinade	457	4.1	2.8	111.5	1229
Percentage of Calories derived from Fats: 5.45%					

ENTREES

	CAL. (GMS)	PROT. (GMS)	FAT (GMS)	SUGAR (GMS)	SODM. (MGS)
Vegetable Medley Quiche	3,083	168.2	207.2	182.7	3156
Percentage of Calories derived from Fats: 60.49%					
Red Bell Pepper Pasta With Scallops And Asparagus	1,730	128.0	40.3	217.2	2663
Percentage of Calories derived from Fats: 20.95%					
Swedish Meatballs	2,916	192.0	189.6	103.7	5591
Percentage of Calories derived from Fats: 58.52%					
Roast Leg of Lamb Provençal	3,428	395.5	155.8	52.6	1513
Percentage of Calories derived from Fats: 40.91%					
Barbecued Flank Steak	2,498	199.0	163.1	72.8	12709
Percentage of Calories derived from Fats: 58.75%					

	CAL. (GMS)	PROT. (GMS)	FAT (GMS)	SUGAR (GMS)	SODM. (MGS)
Balsamic Rosemary Chicken	1,390	217.6	35.6	34.5	604
Percentage of Calories derived from Fats: 23.08%					
Smokey Southwestern Chicken	3,963	334.2	233.6	84.4	4039
Percentage of Calories derived from Fats: 53.05%					
Ground Turkey Loaf	1,152	145.1	33.0	63.3	2160
Percentage of Calories derived from Fats: 25.78%					
Braised Red Cabbage	581	10.0	33.2	58.9	87
Percentage of Calories derived from Fats: 51.42%					
Poached Salmon With Lemon-Dill Cucumber Sauce	2,068	142.6	138.8	25.6	3563
Percentage of Calories derived from Fats: 60.42%					
Grilled Shrimp With Sweet And Sour Thai Dipping Sauce	1,368	97.7	57.0	104.0	2042
Percentage of Calories derived from Fats: 37.50%					

DESSERTS AND SWEETS

	CAL. (GMS)	PROT. (GMS)	FAT (GMS)	SUGAR (GMS)	SODM. (MGS)
Aloha Apple Pie	3,309	28.5	143.9	506.6	1266
Percentage of Calories derived from Fats: 39.15%					
Pineapple Upside-Down Cake	3,385	29.9	155.8	448.1	2071
Percentage of Calories derived from Fats: 41.42%					
Blackberry Supreme Cake	3,286	37.8	118.6	437.5	3332
Percentage of Calories derived from Fats: 32.48%					
Chocolate-Chip Apple Cake	5,342	76.6	253.0	697.7	685
Percentage of Calories derived from Fats: 42.62%					
Fresh Fruit Ambrosia In Pineapple Shells	1,428	19.3	52.8	198.7	604
Percentage of Calories derived from Fats: 33.30%					
Raspberry Couscous Parfait	1,827	25.9	29.7	229.8	157
Percentage of Calories derived from Fats: 14.63%					
Mango Melba Sundae	1,393	24.2	53.7	223.9	208
Percentage of Calories derived from Fats: 34.69%					

	CAL. (GMS)	PROT. (GMS)	FAT (GMS)	SUGAR (GMS)	SODM. (MGS)
Strawberries Yin Yang	329	14.1	5.5	45.2	211
Percentage of Calories derived from Fats: 15.17%					
Fresh Fruit Trifle	4,515	56.6	178.0	624.6	3490
Percentage of Calories derived from Fats: 35.49%					

DESSERT SAUCES

	CAL. (GMS)	PROT. (GMS)	FAT (GMS)	SUGAR (GMS)	SODM. (MGS)
Berry Coulis	782	7.2	6.9	156.8	9
Percentage of Calories derived from Fats: 7.94%					
Mango Coulis	847	5.6	3.3	187.5	61
Percentage of Calories derived from Fats: 3.51%					
Melba Sauce	641	5.0	3.6	150.2	6
Percentage of Calories derived from Fats: 5.05%					
Lemon Sauce	619	0.2	22.6	101.3	9
Percentage of Calories derived from Fats: 32.86%					
Orange Sauce	700	1.4	23.8	114.6	6
Percentage of Calories derived from Fats: 30.57%					

FRUIT SORBETS

	CAL. (GMS)	PROT. (GMS)	FAT (GMS)	SUGAR (GMS)	SODM. (MGS)
Tangerine Sorbet	715	9.3	2.7	186.2	27
Percentage of Calories derived from Fats: 3.35%					
Strawberry, Raspberry or Blackberry Sorbet	302	2.5	2.0	78.9	5
Percentage of Calories derived from Fats: 5.95%					
Lemon Sorbet	432	126.4			
Percentage of Calories derived from Fats: 0.00%					
Mango Sorbet	980	7.0	4.1	227.8	74
Percentage of Calories derived from Fats: 3.77%					
Berry Wine Sorbet	1,064	4.0	3.7	140.5	47
Percentage of Calories derived from Fats: 3.10%					
Fruit And Spice Cookies	4,753	59.7	222.5	522.8	369
Percentage of Calories derived from Fats: 42.13%					
Carrot Raisin Muffins	1,618	43.0	47.6	196.0	3089
Percentage of Calories derived from Fats: 26.47%					

JUICE YIELDS

FRUITS	QUANTITY	YIELD
Grapefruit	1	1/2 cup (4 oz)
Lemons	1	2 tablespoons
Limes	1	1 tablespoon
Orange	1	1/4 cup plus
Tangerines	1	3 tablespoons
Kumquats	8-10	1/4 cup (2 oz)
Apples	1 medium	1/4 cup
Apricots	1 pound (9)	1 cup
Cherries	1 pound	11 ounces
Cranberries	3 cups	1/2 cup
Grapes	1 cup, no stems	1/2 cup
Kiwi	1	2 tablespoons
Mango	1	3 ounces *
Nectarines	3	6 ounces
Papaya	1	1/2 cup
Peaches	1 large	1/2 cup
Pears	1 large	3/4 cup
Pineapple	1 small	5 ounces
Plums	1 pound (5)	6 ounces
Prunes	not recommended	
Pomegranate	1/2 cup seeds	1/4 cup juice
Blackberries	1 box (demi sec)	1/2 cup
Olallieberries	1 box	1/2 cup
Blueberries	1/2 cup	1/4 cup

	QUANTITY	YIELD
Raspberries	1 box (demi sec)	1/2 cup
Strawberries	1 basket	3/4 cup
Cantaloup	1 average	1 cup
Honeydew	1 medium	1 1/4 cups
Watermelon	1/2 melon	2 cups
VEGETABLES		
Beets	3	1/2 cup
Carrots	2 large	3/4 cup
Celery	3 stalks	1/2 cup
Cucumber, garden	1	1/2 cup
Cucumber, English	1	3/4 cup
Leeks	1	2 tablespoons
Lettuce	6 leaves	2 tablespoons
Onions	4 medium	1/2 cup
Parsley	process with other vegetables	
Peppers	1 bell	1/3 cup
Potatoes	1 medium	1/2 cup
Spinach	1 pound	2/3 cup
Tomatoes	3 Italian Plum	3/4 cup
	2 large	3/4 cup

*Juice is thick, almost a purée consistency.

BIBLIOGRAPHY

Ballisister, Barry. *Fruit and Vegetable Stand.* New York: Overlook Press, 1987.

Bonar, Ann. *The Macmillan Treasury of Herbs.* New York: Macmillan Publishing Company, 1985.

California Food and Agricultural Code.

California Health and Safety Code.

Gentry, Patricia. *Kitchen Tools: Cooking with a Twist and a Flair!* Santa Rosa, Calif.: The Cole Group/101 Productions, 1988.

McGee, Harold. *On Food and cooking: The Science and Lore of the Kitchen.* New York: Scribner's, 1984.

INDEX

Pat Gentry is a cooking instructor and owns and operates, with her daughter, a catering company: Michael's of Monterey Bay. A member of the Southern California Culinary Guild, the San Francisco Professional Food Society, and the International Association of Culinary Professionals, she is the author of *Kitchen Tools* and *Teatime Celebrations*.

Lynn Devereux has been both a chef and restaurant owner in California. A native of Missouri, currently she lives in the San Francisco bay area. *Juice It Up!* is her first cookbook.